Texturing Techniques with 3ds Max 2017®: The Ultimate Beginner's Guide

ROC

and

Elizabeth VT

RISING POLYGON

Texturing Techniques with 3ds Max 2017 - The Ultimate Beginner's Guide

Copyright © Rising Polygon

Book Code: RPO5C

Edition: 2nd Edition

ISBN: 978-1539665991

Web: www.risingpolgon.co

Author Email: rconor@risingpolgon.co

Contents

Acknowledgements

About the Author

Preface

Acknowledgements

Thanks to:

Everyone at Autodesk [**www.autodesk.com**].
Everyone at Microsoft [**www.microsoft.com**].

Thanks to all great digital artists who inspire us with their innovative VFX, gaming, animation, and motion graphics content.

And a very special thanks to wonderful CG artists of London, UK.

Finally, thank you for picking up the book.

This page is intentionally left blank

About the Author

Rising Polygon, founded by **Ravi Conor** aka **ROC**, **Elizabeth VT**, and **Gordon Fisher** is a group of like-minded professionals and freelancers who are specialized in advertising, graphic design, web design and development, digital marketing, multimedia, exhibition, print design, branding, and CG content creation.

ROC has over a decade of experience in the computer graphics field and although he is primarily a shading and texturing artist, he is also experienced in the fields of Dynamics, UVMapping, Lighting, and Rendering. Along side 3ds Max, ROC has experience with VRay, Maya, FumeFX, Mudbox, Mari, Photoshop, xNormal, UVLayout, Premiere, and After Effects.

Elizabeth is primarily an Android App developer. She is passionate about computer graphics and has an experience of over 6 years with 3ds Max, Maya, Photoshop, and Blender.

Gordon Fisher is the back bone of Rising Polygon and handles operations, finance, and accounts.

You can contact authors by sending an e-mail to the following Email ID: **rconor@risingpolygon.co.**

This page is intentionally left blank

Preface

Why this Book?

The **Texturing Techniques with 3ds Max 2017 - The Ultimate Beginner's Guide, 2nd Edition** textbook offers a hands-on exercises based strategy for all those digital artists who have just started working on the 3ds Max [no experience needed] and interested in learning texturing in 3ds Max. This brilliant guide takes you step-by-step through the whole process of texturing. From the very first pages, the users of the book will learn how to effectively use 3ds Max for shading surfaces.

What you need?

To complete the examples and hands-on exercises in this book, you need 2017 version of Autodesk 3ds Max.

What are the main features of the book?

*   The book is written using 3ds Max 2017 in an easy to understand language.
*   Shading and texturing techniques covered.
*   31 Hands-on exercises to hone your skills.
*   Detailed coverage of tools and features.
*   Additional tips, guidance, and advice is provided.
*   Important terms are in bold face so that you never miss them.
*   Support for technical aspect of the book.
*   3ds Max files and textures used are available for download from the accompanying website.

Is this book is available in e-Book format?

Yes. You can download the color e-Book from the Amazon's Kindle store.

How This Book Is Structured?

This book is divided into following units:

Unit MI1 - Introduction to 3ds Max - I
*   Navigating the workspace
*   Customizing the interface
*   Understanding various UI components
*   Working with the file management commands

- Setting preferences for 3ds Max
- Understanding workspaces
- Understanding the enhanced menu system
- Working with viewports
- Setting preferences for the viewports
- Creating objects in the scene
- Selecting objects
- Using the navigational gizmos
- Moving, rotating, and scaling objects
- Getting help
- Per-view Preferences, Creative Market Store, Asset Library, Print Studio, and Game Exporter

Unit MI2 - Introduction to 3ds Max - II

- Working with templates
- Creating clones and duplicates
- Understanding hierarchies
- Working with the **Scene** and **Layer** Explorers
- Understanding the **Mirror** tool, the **Select and Place** tool, and the **Select and Manipulate** tool
- Working with the **Align** tool and the **Array** tool
- Working with precision and drawing aids
- Understanding modifiers, and normals

Unit MT1 - Material Editors

- Compact Material Editor
- Slate Material Editor

Unit MT2 - General/Scanline Materials and Maps

- General/Scanline materials
- General maps

Unit MT3 - Physical, mental ray, and Autodesk Materials

- Autodesk Materials
- Arch & Design Material
- Physical Material

Examination Copies

Books received as examination copies are for review purposes only and may not be made available for student use. Resale of the examination copies is prohibited. If you want to receive this book as an examination copy, send the request from your official e-mail id to us using the **Contact** page of from our website.

Electronic Files

Any electronic file associated with this book are licensed to the original user only. These files can not be transferred to a third party. However, the original user can use these files in personal projects without taking any permission from **Rising Polygon**.

Trademarks

3ds Max is the registered trademarks of **Autodesk Inc. Windows** is the registered trademarks of **Microsoft Inc.**

Disclaimer

All rights reserved. No part of this book may be reproduced, stored in a retrieval system, or transmitted in any form or by any means, without the prior written permission of the publisher, except in the case of brief quotations embedded in critical articles or reviews. No patent liability is assumed with respect to the use of information contained herein. Although every precaution has been taken in the preparation of this book, neither the author, nor **Rising Polygon**, and its dealers and distributors will be held liable for any damages caused or alleged to be caused directly or indirectly by this book.

All terms mentioned in this book that are known to be trademarks or service marks have been appropriately capitalized. **Rising Polygon** cannot attest to the accuracy of this information. Use of a term in this book should not be regarded as affecting the validity of any trademark or service mark.

Access to Electronic Files

This book is sold via multiple sales channels. If you don't have access to the resources used in this book, you can place a request for the resources by visiting the following link: *hhttp://bit.ly/resources-rp.*

Customer Support

At **Rising Polygon**, our technical team is always ready to take care of your technical queries. If you are facing any problem with the technical aspect of the book, navigate to *http://bit.ly/contact-rp* and let us know about your query.

Reader Feedback

Your feedback is always welcome. Your feedback is critical to our efforts at **Rising Polygon** and it will help us in developing quality titles in the future. To send the feedback, visit *http://bit.ly/contact-rp.*

Errata

We take every precaution while preparing the content of the book but mistakes do happen. If you find any mistake in this book general or technical, we would be happy that you report it to us so that we can mention it in the errata section of the book's online page. If you find any errata, please report them by visiting the following link: *http://bit.ly/contact-rp*. This will help the other readers from frustration. Once your errata is verified, it will appear in the errata section of the book's online page.

Contact Author

Stay connected with us through Twitter (**@risingpolygon**) to know the latest updates about our products, information about books, and other related information. You can also send an e-mail to author at the following address: **rconor@risingpolygon.co**.

Unit MI1: Introducing 3ds Max - 1

Welcome to the latest version [2017] of **3ds Max**. In any 3D computer graphics application, the first thing you encounter is interface. Interface is where you view and work with your scene. The 3ds Max's interface is intuitive and highly customizable. You can make changes to the interface and then save multiple 3ds Max User Interface [UI] settings using the **Workspaces** feature. You can create multiple workspaces and switch between them easily.

In this release, Autodesk has modernized the interface using streamlined new icons. However, the icons look somewhat similar to the previous version. If you are long time user of 3ds Max, you will not have difficulties in identifying them. Autodesk has also refined the typography for a cleaner look.

In this unit, I'll describe the following:

- Understanding workspaces
- Navigating the workspace
- Customizing the interface
- Understanding various UI components
- Working with the file management commands
- Setting preferences for 3ds Max
- Understanding the enhanced menu system
- Working with viewports
- Setting preferences for the viewports
- Creating objects in the scene
- Selecting objects
- Using the navigational gizmos
- Moving, rotating, and scaling objects
- Getting help
- Per-view Preferences, Creative Market Store, Asset Library, Print Studio, and Game Exporter

Note: Interface Customization

*By default, 3ds Max starts with a dark theme [white text on the dark gray background]. This is good for those digital artists who spend hours working on 3ds Max, however, the default theme is not good for printing. I have customized the theme so that the captures appear fine when book is printed. You can easily switch between the custom color themes from the **Choose initial settings for tool options and UI layout** dialog. To open this dialog, choose **Custom UI and Default Switcher** from the **Customize** menu.*

The 3ds Max's interface is now **HDPI** [High Dots Per Inch] aware. Now, Windows scaling is correctly applied when interface appears on high DPI monitors and laptops. If you are working on a ultra-high resolution monitor, the 3ds Max's icons may appear small. You can scale the interface from the Windows control panel. Here's the process on Windows 7.

RMB click on your **Desktop** and choose **Screen Resolution** from the popup menu. On the window displayed, choose **Make text and other items larger or smaller**. Now, you can choose a preset value from the page [see Figure F1]. If you want to create a custom text size, click **Set custom size (DPI)** from the left of the page [see Figure F1]. Now, click drag the scale on the **Custom DPI Setting** dialog to change the scale [see Figure F2]. Click **OK** to accept the settings.

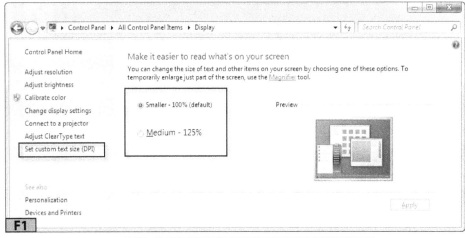

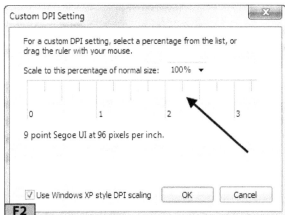

When you first time open the 3ds Max application, you will see the **Select your initial 3ds Max experience** window [see Figure F3]. You can set default template for your 3ds Max scenes from this window. Select the desired template and then click **Continue** to open the default workspace with the **Welcome Screen** [see Figure F4]. There are three panels available in the **Welcome Screen: Learn, Start**, and **Extend**.

The content of the **Start** panel appears by default in the **Welcome Screen**. From the **RECENT FILES** section of this panel, you can open the recent files you have worked on. Also, you can look for files on your storage device by clicking the **Browse** button. On the right of the **Start** panel, you will see some templates in the **START-UP TEMPLATES** section and a link to open the **Template Manager**. You can use the **Template Manager** to inspect and edit existing templates.

F3

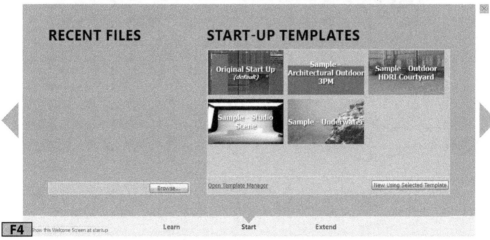

F4

To create a new scene, choose a template and then click **New Using Selected Template**. A new scene will be created with the settings specified by that template. I will explain templates in details in the **Unit MI2**. The **Learn** panel [see Figure F5] contains list of **1-Minute Startup Movies** that you can view to learn the basics of some 3ds Max features. When you select a movie from the list, you are taken to a web page where the movie is being played. In the **More Learning Resources** section, there are four links for navigating to 3ds Max Learning Channel, what's new page, learning path page, and downloading the sample content.

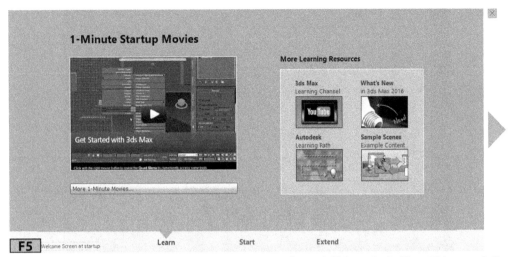

F5   Welcome Screen at startup   Learn   Start   Extend

The **Extend** panel [see Figure F6] features ways to extend capabilities of 3ds Max. This panel displays featured apps from the **Autodesk Exchange Store**. It also contains list of useful Autodesk resources.

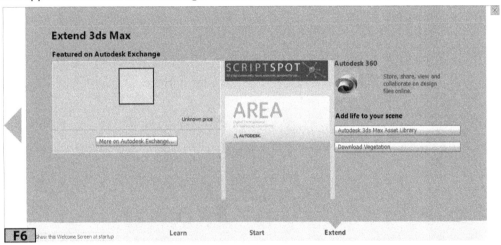

F6   Show this Welcome Screen at startup   Learn   Start   Extend

Note: Welcome Screen
*If you don't want to see the **Welcome Screen** when next time you open 3ds Max, turn off **Show this Welcome Screen at startup**. You can bring back the screen anytime by choosing **Welcome Screen** from the **Help** menu.*

Close the **Welcome Screen** to view the default UI of 3ds Max [refer Figure F7].

Notice, I have marked different components of the UI with numbers to make the learning process easier. In 3ds Max, commands and tools are arranged in groups so that you can find them easily. For example, all viewport navigation tools are grouped together on the bottom-right corner of the interface [marked as 12 in Figure F7]. The 3ds Max interface can be divided into 12 sections. I have marked those sections in Figure F7. Table 1 summarizes the numbers and the sections of the UI they represent.

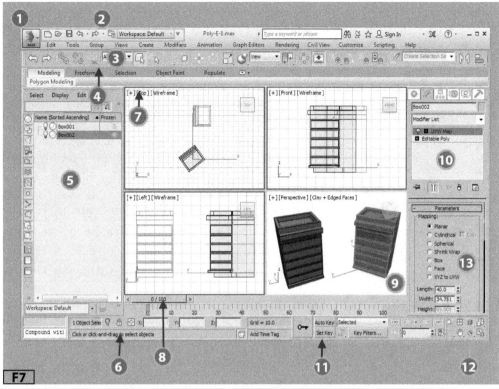

F7

Table 1: 3ds Max interface overview

No.	Item	Description
1	Application Button	On clicking this button, the **Application** menu appears. This menu contains file management commands.
2	Quick Access Toolbar	This toolbar gives access to the file handling and undo/redo commands. It also contains a drop-down that lets you switch among different workspaces.
3	Main Toolbar	This toolbar provides many commonly used tools.
4	The Ribbon	The **Ribbon** contains many tools for modeling and painting in the scene. Also, here you will find tools for adding people to populate a scene.
5	Scene Explorer	The **Scene Explorer** lets you view, sort, filter, and select objects in a scene. You can also use it to rename, delete, hide, and freeze objects. It is also used to create and amend object hierarchies.
6	Status Bar Controls	The **Status Bar** contains the prompt and status information about the scene. The Coordinate Transform Type-In boxes in the **Status Bar** let you transform the objects manually.

7	Viewport Label Menus	These menus let you change the shading style for the viewport. They also contain other viewport related commands and features.
8	Time Slider	Allows you to navigate along the timeline.
9	Viewports	Viewports let you view your scene from multiple angles. They also allow you to preview lighting, shading, shadows, and other effects.
10	Command Panel	The **Command Panel** is the nerve center of 3ds Max. It contains six panels that you can use to create and modify objects in 3ds Max.
11	Create and Play Back Animation	These controls affect the animation. This area also contains buttons to playback animation in the viewports.
12	Viewport Navigation	These buttons allow you to navigate your scene [Active Viewport].
13	Rollout	Rollouts are used to change properties of the object in 3ds Max.

There are some other elements of the interface that are not visible in the default UI. These elements appear when you run a command from the **Main** toolbar or menu, or choose an option from the RMB click menu. Here's is the quick rundown to those elements:

■ **Floating Toolbars**: There are quite a few floating toolbars available in 3ds Max. To access these toolbar, RMB click on a gray area on the toolbar to open a popup menu [see Figure F8] containing the options for invoking the floating toolbars. The popup menu shown in Figure F8 displayed when I RMB clicked on the gray area below the **Named Selection Sets** drop-down on the **Main** toolbar. The area is marked with an arrow in Figure F8. When I chose **MassFx Toolbar** from the popup menu, the floating **Mass FX Toolbar** appeared [see Figure F9].

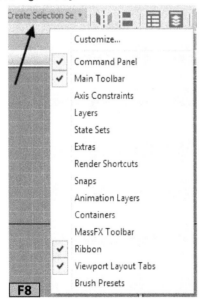

■ **Quad Menus**: Whenever you RMB click in an active viewport [except on a viewport label], 3ds Max opens a **Quad** menu at the location of the mouse pointer. The **Quad** menu can display up to four quadrants [see Figure F10] with various commands and allows you to work efficiently as the commands in the menu are context-sensitive. The **Quad** menu is the quickest way to find commands.

Figure F10 shows a **Quad** menu which appeared when I RMB clicked on an **Editable Poly** object in the viewport.

■ **Caddy Controls**: A caddy control in 3ds Max can be described as **"in-canvas"** interface that comprises a dynamic label and an array of buttons superimposed over a viewport. You can use the standard mouse operations such as clicking and dragging to change the values in the spinners.

The changes you made are immediately updated in the viewport. The **Chamfer** caddy control shown in Figure F11 appeared when I selected edges of a box and then clicked **Chamfer's** settings button on the **Command Panel**.

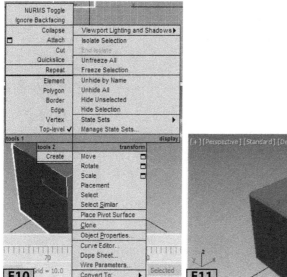

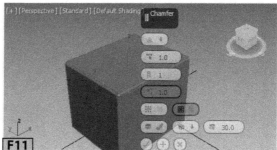

■ **Dialogs, Windows, and Editors**: Some of the commands in 3ds Max opens dialogs, editors, and windows. Some of these elements have their own menu bars and toolbars. Figure F12 shows the **Slate Material Editor**. You can use the **M** hotkey to open this editor.

Note: Spinners

*Spinners are found everywhere in 3ds Max [I have marked **U** and **V** spinners with black rectangle in Figure F12]. Spinners are controllers that you will touch on regular basis. They allow you to quickly amend numerical values with ease. To change the value in a spinner, click the up or down arrow on the right of the spinner. To change values quickly, click and drag the arrows. You can also type a value directly in the spinner's field.*

Tip: Fast and slow scroll rate in a spinner

*Press and hold **Alt** and then click-drag the spinner's up or down arrow for a slower numerical scroll rate. Hold **Ctrl** for the faster scroll rate. RMB click on a spinner to set it to its default value.*

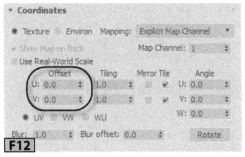

F12

Note: Numerical Expression Evaluator

*If the type cursor is located inside a spinner and you press **Ctrl+N**, the **Numerical Expression Evaluator** appears [see Figure F13]. This evaluator lets you calculate the value for the spinner using an expression. For example, if you type **30+50** in this evaluator's field and click **Paste**, 80 appears in the associated spinner.*

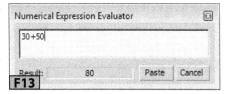

F13

Note: Modeless dialogs, controls, windows, and editors

*Quite a few dialogs in 3ds Max are **modeless** meaning the dialog doesn't need to be closed in order to work on other elements of the interface. A good example of modeless dialog is the **Slate Material Editor**. You can minimize the editor and continue working on the scene. Other modeless dialogs that you would frequently use are **Transform Type-In** dialogs, **Caddy** controls, **Render Scene** dialog, and so forth.*

Tip: Toggling the visibility of all open dialogs
*You can toggle visibility of all open dialogs by using the **Ctrl+~** hotkeys.*

UI Components
The following section presents what you need to know about 3ds Max UI.

Caption Bar
The **Caption** bar is another name for the **Title** bar. It is the topmost element in the 3ds Max UI [see Figure F14].

F14

The **Title** bar hosts the **Application** button, **Quick Access Toolbar**, **Workspaces** drop-down, and **InfoCenter**. It also displays the name of the current 3ds Max file.

Quick Access Toolbar
This toolbar provides most commonly used file-management commands as well as commands for **Undo** and **Redo**. It also contains a drop-down that allows you to switch between different workspaces. Table 2 summarizes the interface of the **Quick Access Toolbar**.

Table 2: The **Quick Access Toolbar** interface		
Item	**Icon**	**Description**
New Scene	▢	Click to create a new scene.

Open File	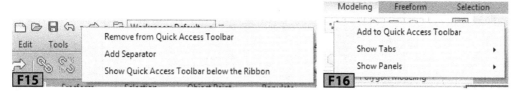	Click to open a saved file from the storage.
Save File		Click to save file to the disk.
Undo Scene Operation		Click to undo the previous operation. Click the arrow on the right of the button to open a list of previous operations performed in the scene. Hotkeys: **Ctrl+Z**.
Redo Scene Operation		Click to redo the previous operation. Hotkeys: **Ctrl+Y**.
Project Folder		Click to open the **Browse For Folder** dialog to set a project folder for the scene.
Workspaces drop-down list	Workspace: Default	Click to open the options available for managing and switching workspaces.
Quick Access toolbar drop-down		Click to display options to manage the **Quick Access Toolbar**.

Q. Can I remove a button from the Quick Access Toolbar?

Yes. RMB click on a button on the toolbar and then choose **Remove from Quick Access Toolbar** [see Figure F15]. You can also add any button from the **Ribbon** to the **Quick Access Toolbar** by RMB clicking on the button and then choosing **Add To Quick Access Toolbar** [see Figure F16].

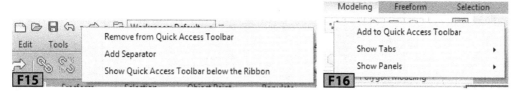

Q. Is there any place in the UI from where I can access file management commands?

Yes. You can access file management commands from the **Application** menu. To open the menu, click the **Application** button. You can also open the menu using the **Alt+F** hotkeys. When you press **Alt+F**, 3ds Max superimposes hotkeys on the corresponding **Application** menu items [see Figure F17].

Now, for example, if you want to reset the scene, press **Atl+F+R**. To open the **Preferences** dialog, press **Alt+F+C**. To exit 3ds Max, press **Alt+F+X**.

Q. What's the function of the Reset command?

This command clears all data as well resets 3ds Max settings such as viewport configuration, snap settings, **Material Editor**, background image, and so forth. If you have done some customization during the current session of the 3ds Max, and you execute the **Reset** command, all startup defaults will be restored according to the setting stored in the **maxstrat.max** file.

Q. How can I use maxstart.max?

You can use this file to make the changes you would like to see at the startup. Start 3ds Max and make the adjustments. Then, save file in the **scenes** folder with the name **maxstrat.max**.

Note: Templates
If you reset the scene, it will also affect the template that you had used to open the scene. The template will be reset back to its default settings.

Q. How can I change the undo levels?
You can change it from the **Preferences** dialog. By default, 3ds Max allows only **20** levels for the undo operations. To change it, choose **Preferences** from the **Customize** menu. On the **General** panel of the dialog, you can set **Levels** from the **Scene Undo** group.

Q. What's the use of the Preferences dialog?
The **Preferences** dialog contains options that 3ds Max offers for its operations. 3ds Max behaves according to the options you set in the **Preferences** dialog. You have just seen an example how you can change the undo levels. If you increase the number of levels, you force 3ds Max to obey that setting. The **Preferences** dialog comprises many panels with lots of options that you can use.

Tip: The Preferences dialog
*You can also open the **Preferences** dialog by clicking **Options** from the **Application** menu.*

Q. Can I undo all commands in 3ds Max?

No. You cannot undo commands such as saving a file or using the **Collapse** utility. If you know an action cannot be undone, first hold you scene by choosing **Hold** from the **Edit** menu [Hotkeys: **Ctrl+H**]. When you want to recall, choose **Fetch** from the **Edit** menu [Hotkeys: **Alt+Ctrl+F**].

Q. Why do I need a project folder?

When you work on a project, you have to deal with many scenes, texture files, third party data, rendering, material libraries, and so forth. If you don't organize the data for the project, it would be very difficult for you to manage the assets for the project. The project folder allows you to organize all your files in a folder for a particular project. You can also set a project by choosing **Manage | Set Project Folder** from the **Application** menu.

Q. What is the Workspaces feature?

This feature allows you to quickly switch between the different arrangement of panels, toolbars, menus, viewports, and other interface elements. Figure F18 shows the UI when **Default with Enhanced Menu** workspace is chosen. Choose **Reset To Default State** from the **Workspaces** drop-down to rest the workspace to the saved settings of the active workspace. On choosing the **Manage Workspaces** from the **Workspaces** drop-down, the **Manage Workspaces** dialog appears [see Figure F19] from where you can switch, add, edit, and delete workspaces.

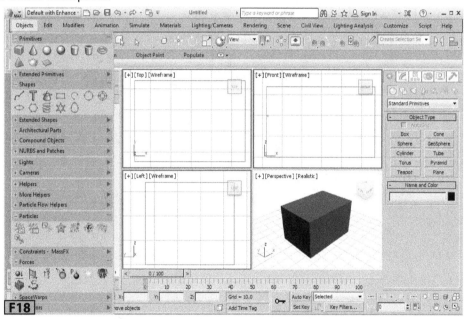

F18

Q. What are enhanced menus?

3ds Max offers two types of menu systems for the menu bar: **Standard** menu [default] and the **Enhanced** menu. The menu bar is located directly under the main interface window's **Title** bar.

The default menu system follows the standard **Windows** conventions. When you click on a menu item on the menu bar, a pulldown menu appears. The menu in Figure F17 appeared when I clicked **Edit** on the menu bar. Notice that hotkeys are displayed next to some of the commands. You can use these hotkeys to execute the command without invoking the menu. For example, to select all objects in a scene, you can press **Ctrl+A**. Not all the commands are available all the time. These commands are context-sensitive. If a command is not available, it is grayed out in the menu, for example, see the **Fetch** command in Figure F20. If a black triangle appears [for example, the **Selection Region** command in the **Edit** menu] on the next to a menu command, it indicates that a sub-menu exists. Place the mouse pointer on the command to view the sub-menu.

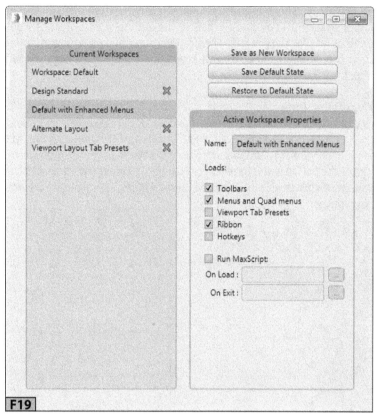

F19

Tip: Menu hotkey
*You can use the keyboard [Alt key] to invoke a pulldown menu. Press **Alt**, 3ds Max displays the hotkey with an underline for the menu items. For example, to invoke the **Edit** pull-down menu, press **Alt+E**. Similarly, for the **Customize** menu, press **Alt+U**.*

Tip: Hiding menu bar
*If for some reason, you want to hide the menu bar, RMB click on the menu bar then click **Show Menu Bar** from the pop-up menu. To recover the menu back, click on the arrow located on the right of the **Workspaces** drop-down [see Figure F21] and then choose **Show Menu Bar**. You can also hide menu bar from the **Quick Access Toolbar** menu.*

The **Enhanced** menu system provides some additional features such as configurable display, link to relevant help topics, enhanced tool tips, and drag and drop menu categories. You can also search for the menu commands. The image at the left of Figure F22 shows standard **Rendering** menu whereas the image at the right of Figure F22 shows enhanced **Rendering** menu.

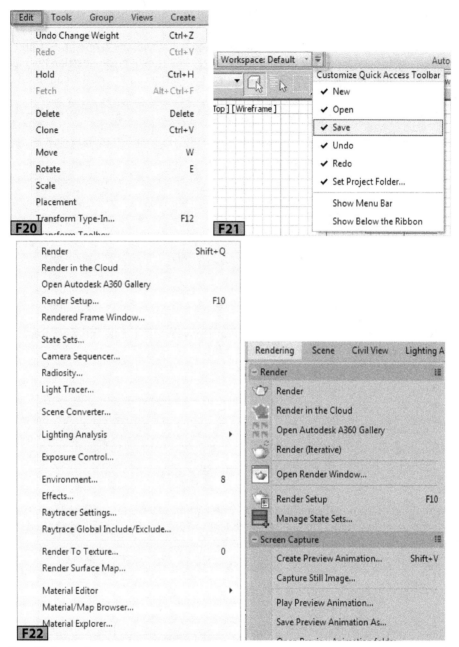

F20
F21
F22

Tip: Toggling Enhanced menu

*You can toggle the enhanced menu by using the **Enhanced Menu** command. To access this command, press **X** to open the **Search All Action** dialog and then type **enh** in the field available in this dialog [see Figure F23]. The **Enhanced Menus** command appears in the list. Click it to open the enhanced menu sytem.*

Here's is a quick run down to the various functions available for the **Enhanced** menu system:

■ You can collapse or expand each panel in a menu. When collapsed, a **+** icon appears on the title bar. When expanded a **-** icon appears on the title bar [refer Figure F24]. When you position the mouse pointer on the title bar of a collapsed menu, a sub-menu appears with the content of the collapsed menu [refer Figure F24].

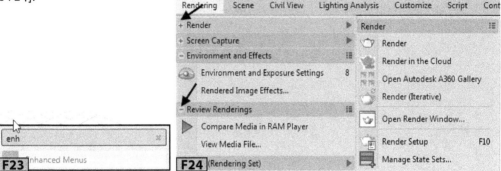

Note: Restoring menu settings
3ds Max remembers all settings of collapsed or expanded states of the menu and it restores them when you reopen 3ds Max.

■ You can view the content of a menu as icon, text, or icon+text. To toggle the view mode, click on the icon at the top-right end of the title bar [see Figure F25].

■ To view the detailed tooltip that provides a brief description of a menu command, position the mouse pointer on the menu option, a tool tip appears [see Figure F26]. If you want to see help documentation about the command under the mouse pointer, press **F1**.

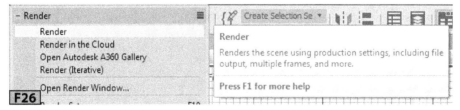

■ You can also float a menu panel or submenu. Drag the title bar of the panel away from the menu to make it a floating panel [see Figure F27].

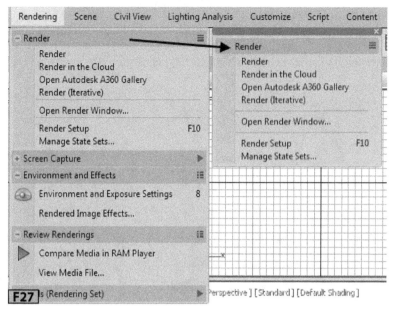

F27

■ You can also merge the floating panels. Drag title bar of a panel to the bottom or top of the target panel, a blue line appears [see the image at the left of Figure F28]. Release the mouse button to dock the two panels [see the image at the right of Figure F28].

■ You can also search a menu command from the menu. Type the name of the command when the menu is active. A text box appears at top of the menu when you start typing. As you type, menu shows the command matching with the string you have typed [see Figure F29].

F28   F29

Viewports

In 3ds Max, you will be doing most of the work in viewports. Viewports are openings into 3D space you work. A viewport represents 3D space using the **Cartesian** coordinates system. The coordinate are expressed using three numbers such as **[10, 10, 20]**. These number represent points in 3D space. The origin is always at **[0, 0, 0]**. By default, 3ds Max displays a four viewport arrangement: **Top**, **Front**, **Left**, and **Perspective**. The **Top**, **Front**, and **Left** are known as orthographic views. 3ds Max provides many options to change the viewport as well as the layout. Using multiple viewports can help you visualize the scene better.

Q. What do you mean by an Orthographic View?

Most of the 3D designs created using computer relies on the 2D representation of the designs. Some examples of the 2D representations are maps, elevations, and plans. Even to create a character model, you first design it on paper [front, side, and back views] [see Figure F30] and then create 3D model using these designs.

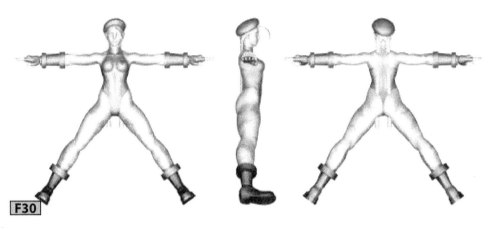

F30

Note:

Blueprint Courtesy: *http://www.the-blueprints.com*

In laymen terms, you can think of the orthographic views as flat, or straight on. The orthographic views are two dimensional views. Each dimension is defined by two world coordinate axes. Combination of these two axes produce three sets of orthographic views: **Top and Bottom**, **Front and Back**, and **Left and Right**. Figure F31 shows a model in three orthographic views [**Top**, **Right**, and **Left**] and in **Perspective** view.

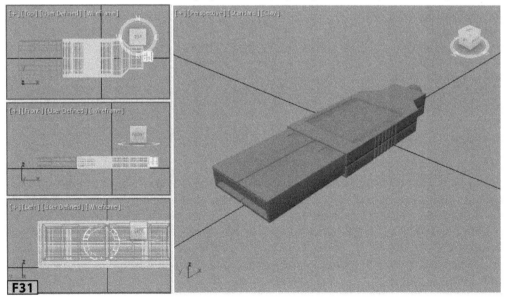

F31

You can change a viewport to various orthographic views using the controls available in the **Point-Of-View (POV)** viewport label menu. The **Perspective** view on the other hand closely resembles with the human view. In 3ds Max there are three ways to create a perspective view: Perspective view, camera view, and light view.

Q. Can you tell me little more about Viewport Label menus and how can I change a viewport to the orthographic views?

Notice on top-left corner of a viewport, there are three labels. Figure F32 shows labels on the **Perspective** viewport. Each label is clickable [click or RMB click]. When you click on any of the labels, a popup menu appears.

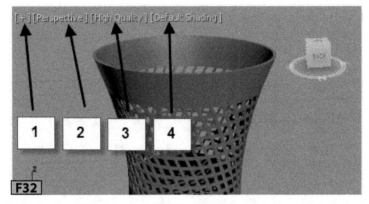

The left most menu is the **General Viewport** label menu [marked as 1], in the middle is the **Point-Of-View [POV]** viewport label menu [marked as 2], and on the right is **Lights and Shadows** viewport label menu [marked as 3]. The right most menu is the **Shading** viewport label menu [marked as 4]. The **General Viewport** label menu comprises controls for overall viewport display or activation. It also gives you access to the **Viewport Configuration** dialog. The **POV Viewport** label menu provides options mainly for changing the viewports. To change a viewport, for example, to change the **Top** viewport to **Bottom** viewport, make sure the **Top** viewport is active and then click or RMB click on the **POV Viewport** label menu. Now, choose **Bottom** from the menu. You can also use the hotkey **B**. Table 3 summarizes the hotkeys that you can use to change the viewports.

Table 3: The hotkeys for switching the viewports	
View	**Hotkey**
Top	T
Bottom	B
Front	F
Left	L
Camera	C
Orthographic	U
Perspective	P

The **Lights and Shadows** menu lets you adjust the behavior of the lights and shadows in the viewport. You can also adjust quality settings from this menu.

The **Shading Viewport** menu lets you control how objects are displayed in the viewport. I will discuss the options in this menu later in the unit.

Q. What is active viewport?

An active viewport is where all actions take place in 3ds Max. One viewport is always active in 3ds Max marked with a highlighted border. To switch the active viewport, you can use any of the three mouse buttons. It is recommended that you use the middle mouse button for making a viewport active as LMB and RMB clicks are also associated with other command in 3ds Max.

When viewports are not maximized, you can press the **Windows** key and **Shift** on the keyboard to cycle the active viewport. When one of the view is maximized, pressing **Windows** key and **Shift** displays the available viewports [see Figure F33] and then you can press **Shift** repeatedly with the **Windows** key held down to cycle among viewports. When you release the keys, the chosen viewport becomes the maximized viewport.

You can save an active viewport in the internal buffer and later restore it. It useful when you want to frame a shot in any view other than a camera view. One view each can be saved for the following viewports: **Top**, **Bottom**, **Left**, **Right**, **Front**, **Back**, **Orthographic**, and **Perspective**. To save an active view, for example the **Perspective** view, activate it with the zoom level you want to save and then choose **Save Active Perspective View** from the **Views** menu. To restore the view, make the **Perspective** view active and then choose **Restore Active Perspective View** from the **Views** menu. The saved active view is saved with the scene file.

Q. How can I change the viewport configuration like the one shown in Figure F31?

The **Viewport Layouts** bar lets you quickly switch among different types of viewport layouts. This bar generally docked on the left of the viewports [see Figure F34]. If it is not visible, RMB click on the **Main** toolbar and then choose **Viewport Layout Tabs** [see Figure F35]. To change the layout, click on the arrow on the bar to open a flyout and then click on the desired layout to make it active. You can also change the layout using the **General Viewport** label menu. Click on the label and then choose **Configure Viewports**. The **Viewport Configuration** dialog appears [see Figure F36]. Select the **Layout** panel and then choose the desired layout. Now, click **OK** to accept the changes.

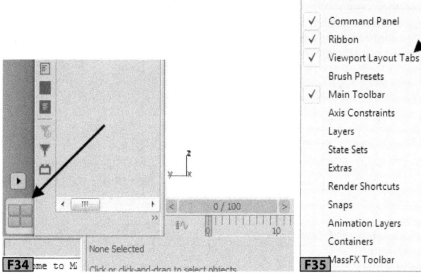

F34

F35

Customize...

✓ Command Panel
✓ Ribbon
✓ Viewport Layout Tabs
   Brush Presets
✓ Main Toolbar
   Axis Constraints
   Layers
   State Sets
   Extras
   Render Shortcuts
   Snaps
   Animation Layers
   Containers
   MassFX Toolbar

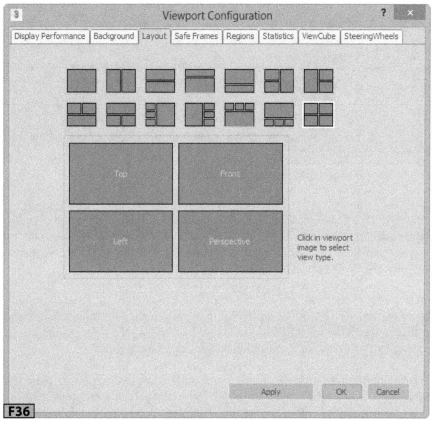

F36

Q. I can see a grid in each viewport, how can I use it?

The grid you see in each viewport is one of the three planes [along the X, Y, and Z axes] that intersect at the right angles to each other at a common point called **origin** [X=0, Y=0, and Z=0]. The three planes based on the world coordinate axes are called **home grid**. To help you easily position objects on the grid, one plane of the home grid is visible in each viewport. The grid acts as a construction plane when you create objects on it.

Tip: Turning off grid

*You can turn off the grid in the active viewport by pressing the **G** hotkey.*

Command Panel

The **Command Panel** is the nerve center of 3ds Max. It comprises of six panels that give you access to most of the modeling tools, animation features, display choices, and utilities. Table 4 summarizes the panels in the **Command Panel**.

Table 4: Different panels in the **Command Panel**	
Panel	**Description**
Create	Contains controls for creating object such as geometry, lights, cameras, and so forth.
Modify	Contains controls for editing objects as well as for applying modifiers to the objects.
Hierarchy	Contains controls for managing links in the hierarchy, joints, and inverse kinematics.
Motion	Contains controls for animation controllers and trajectories.
Display	Contains controls that lets you hide/unhide objects. It also contains display options.
Utilities	Contains different utility programs.

Rollouts

Most of the controls in the **Command Panel** live inside rollouts. A rollout is a group of controls, a section of the **Command Panel** that shows parameters of the selected object. You can collapse the rollouts. When you collapse them, only the title bar of the rollout appears. Figure F37 shows the **Parameters** rollout of the **Box** primitive in the **Modify** panel of the **Command Panel**.

Once you create a box in the viewport, you can modify its parameters such as **Length** and **Width** using the **Parameters** rollout. Each rollout has a title bar that you can click to collapse or expand the rollout. You can also change the default position of the rollout by dragging the dots located on the right of the title and dropping on another place when a blue line appears [see Figure F38].

By default, the rollout occupies a single column space in UI. However, you can increase the numbers of columns by dragging the left most edge of the panel. You can create as many columns as you want [see Figure 35] as long the screen real state is available. Multiple columns are helpful when you are working with an object with which many rollouts are associated.

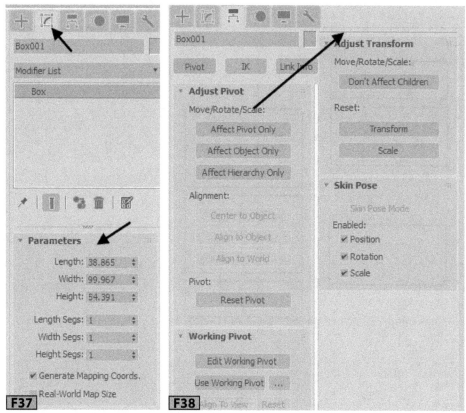

F37 F38

If you RMB click on a rollout [**on the empty gray area**], a popup menu appears [see Figure F39]. This popup allows you to open or close all rollouts at once, or close the rollout on which you RMB clicked.

In the bottom section of the popup menu, you will see a list of rollouts available for the selected object. No tick appears for the collapsed rollouts.

If you have changed order of the rollouts, you can rest the order by choosing **Reset Rollout Order** from the bottom of the menu.

If you have expanded the **Command Panel** to more than one column and you RMB click on a rollout, only those rollouts appear on the popup menu that are in the column [see Figure F40].

Tip: The default value for the spinners
*The nature of the spinners in 3ds Max is persistence meaning that value specified for the spinners remains set for the current spinners. For example, if you created a **Sphere** primitive with **64** segments. When you create the next sphere, the value **64** will be default for it. To reset spinners to their default values, choose **Reset** from the **Application** menu.*

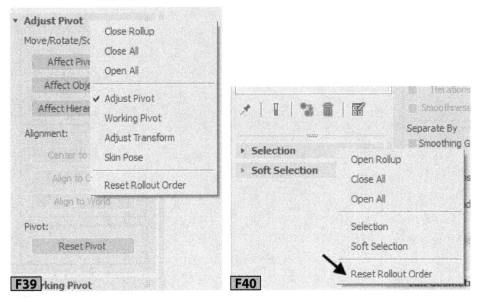

F39 king Pivot   **F40**

Main Toolbar

The **Main** toolbar comprises commonly used tools and dialog. Table 5 summarizes the tools available in the **Main** toolbar.

Table 5: The **Main** toolbar interface overview		
Item	**Icon**	**Description**
Undo/Redo		Undo reverses the last command. Redo reverses the last undo command.
Select and Link		Defines the hierarchical relationship [links] between two objects.
Unlink Selection		Removes the hierarchical relationship between two objects.
Bind to Space Warp		Attaches the current selection to a space warp or vice versa.
Selection Filter List		Limits the selection to specific types and combinations of objects.

Select Object		Selects objects and sub-objects. Hotkey: **Q**.
Select by Name		Allows you to select specific objects from a list of objects using the **Select from Scene** dialog. **Hotkey: H.**
Selection Region Flyout		Allows you to select objects within a region using different methods. You can create different marquee shapes using the options available in this flyout.
Window/Crossing Selection Toggle		Switch between window and crossing methods for selection.
Select and Move		Selects and moves objects. Hotkey: **W**.
Select and Rotate		Selects and rotates objects. Hotkey: **E**.
Select and Scale		Selects and scales objects. Hotkey: **R** to cycle.
Select and Place Flyout		Position an object accurately on the surface of another object.
Reference Coordinate System		Specifies the coordinate system used for a transformations (Move, Rotate, and Scale).

Use Center Flyout		Specifies geometric centers for scale and rotate transformations.
Select and Manipulate		Select objects and allows editing of the parameters for certain objects, modifiers, and controllers by dragging "manipulators" in viewports.
Keyboard Shortcut Override Toggle		Allows you to toggle between using only the "Main User Interface" hotkeys or using both the main hotkeys and hotkeys for groups such as Edit/Editable Mesh, Track View, NURBS, and so on.
2D Snap, 2.5D Snap, 3D Snap		Specify the snap types. Hotkey: **S** to cycle.
Angle Snap Toggle		Enables angle increment snap for rotation. It allows you to snap rotations to certain angles. Hotkey: **A**.
Percent Snap Toggle		Toggles increments scaling of objects by the specified percentage. Hotkeys: **Shift+Ctrl+P**.
Spinner Snap Toggle		Sets the single-click increment or the decrement value for all of the spinners in 3ds Max.
Edit Named Selection Sets		Displays the **Edit Named Selections** dialog, letting you manage named selection sets of sub-objects
Named Selection Sets	Create Selection Se ▼	Allows you to name a selection set and recall the selection for later use.
Mirror		Enables you to move and clone selected objects while reflecting their orientation.
Align Flyout		Gives you access to six different tools for alignment. Hotkeys: Align [**Alt+A**], and Normal Align [**Alt+N**].

Toggle Scene Explorer		Toggles the **Scene Explorer**.
Toggle Layer Explorer		Toggles the **Layer Explorer**.
Toggle Ribbon		Expands or collapses the **Ribbon**.
Curve Editor (Open)		Opens the **Track View - Curve Editor**.
Schematic View (Open)		Opens the **Schematic View** window.
Material Editor flyout		Opens the **Material Editor** that provides functions to create and edit materials and maps.
Render Setup		Opens the **Render Setup** dialog. Hotkey: **F10**.
Rendered Frame Window		Opens the **Rendered Frame Window** that displays rendered output.
Render Production		Renders the scene using the current production render settings without opening the **Render Setup** dialog.
Render Iterative		Renders the scene in iterative mode without opening the **Render Setup** dialog.
ActiveShade		Creates an **ActiveShade** rendering in a floating window.
Render in the cloud		Uses the **A360 Cloud** to render your scene.
Open Autodesk A360 Gallery		Opens a web page that showcases **A360 Cloud** renderings.

Docking and Floating Toolbars

3ds Max allows you to dock and float toolbars. You have already seen an example of the floating toolbar [**Mass FX Toolbar**]. By default, the **Main** toolbar is docked below the menu bar. If you want to undock it, position the mouse pointer in the double vertical lines located at the extreme left of the **Main** toolbar [also available at the extreme right]; the shape of the mouse pointer changes [see Figure F41]. Now, click and drag away and drop when the shape of the mouse pointer changes to a window icon [see Figure F42] to float the **Main** toolbar. Once the toolbar appears as a floating panel [see Figure F43], you can resize it as you resize any other panel on **Windows** operating system.

You can doc the **Main** toolbar back to its last position by double clicking on the title of the floating panel. Similarly, you can float any toolbar, window, or panel [like **Command Panel**, **Scene Explorer**, and **Ribbon**] in 3ds Max.

Tip: Main toolbar visibility toggle
*You can quickly toggle the display of the **Main** toolbar by using the **Alt+6** hotkeys.*

If you RMB click on the title of a floating toolbar, window, or panel. Or, on the vertical or horizontal lines of a toolbar, window, or panel; a pop menu appears with the options to doc that element [see Figure F44].

These options allow you to doc an element on the top, bottom, left, or the right of the interface. However, you can rearrange the interface elements as per you need. For example, if you are a leftie, you would like the **Command Panel** on the left and the **Scene Explorer** on the right. For example, to doc the **Command Panel** on the left, position the mouse pointer on the top right corner of the panel until the shape of the pointer changes [see Figure F45].

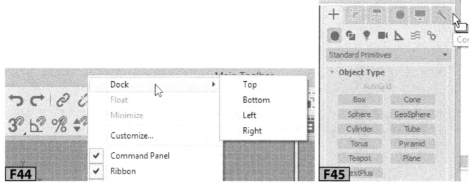

Drag the **Command Panel** to the left of the **Scene Explorer** when the shape of the cursor changes to the one shown in Figure F46 to doc the **Command Panel** on the left [see Figure F47].

Tip: Resetting Workspace
After experimenting with the rearrangement of panels, you can reset the original positions of the elements by choosing
***Reset to Default State** from the **Workspaces** drop-down.*

Note: Quick Access Toolbar
*The **Quick Access Toolbar** and **InfoCenter** toolbar cannot be undocked from the 3ds Max UI.*

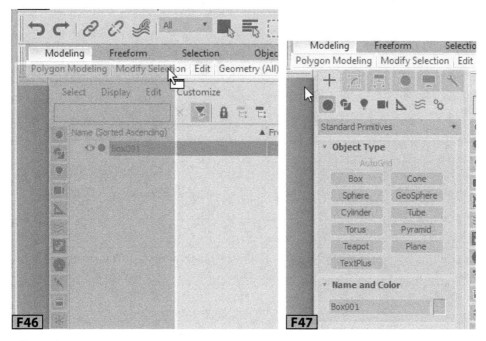

F46 F47

Main Toolbar Flyouts

You might have noticed a small triangle on the lower right corner of some buttons in the **Main** toolbar. Click on hold on such a button to expand a flyout with additional buttons. Figure F48 shows the **Selection Region** flyout.

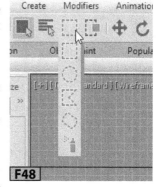

F48

Ribbon

Ribbon [see Figure F49], is available below the **Main** toolbar. The **Ribbon** appears in collapsed state by default. To expand it, double-click on it. You can toggle the display of the **Ribbon** by clicking **Toggle Ribbon** from the **Main** toolbar.

It contains many tabs. The content in the tabs is depended on the context. The items displayed may vary according to the selected sub-objects. I will cover **Ribbon** in a later unit in the book.

F49

Most of the tools are only visible in the **Ribbon** when you are editing a poly object. You will learn about **Ribbon** and poly modeling techniques in a later unit.

Animation and Time Controls

The animation controls are found on the left of the **Viewport Navigation** controls [see Figure F50].

Two other controls that are vital to animation are **Time Slider** and **Track Bar** [see Figure F51]. These controls are available below the viewports. The **Time Slider** works with the **Track Bar** to allow you to view and edit animation. The sliders shows the current frame and the total number of frames in the range. The **Track Bar** shows the frame numbers and allows you to move, copy, and delete keys.

F50 **F51**

Table 6 summarizes the animation controls.

Table 6: The animation controls

Item	Icon	Description
Auto Key Animation Mode, Set Key Animation Mode		The Auto Key Animation Mode toggles the keyframing mode called **Auto Key**. Set Key Animation Mode allows you to create keys for selected objects individual tracks using a combination of the **Set Keys** button and **Key Filters**.
Selection List		Provides quick access to **Named Selection Sets** and track sets.
Default In/Out Tangents for New Keys		This flyout provides a quick way to set a default tangent type for new animation keys.
Key Filters		Opens the **Set Key Filters** dialog where you can specify the tracks on which keys are created.
Go To Start		Moves the time slider to the first frame of the active time segment.
Previous Frame/Key		Moves the time slider back one frame.
Play/Stop		The Play button plays the animation in the active viewport. You can stop the playback by clicking on the button again.
Next Frame/Key		Moves the time slider ahead one frame.
Go To End		Moves the time slider to the last frame of the active time segment.
Current Frame (Go To Frame)		Displays the number or time of the current frame, indicating the position of the time slider.
Key Mode		Allows you jump directly between keyframes in your animation.
Time Configuration		Open the **Time Configuration** dialog that allows you to specify the settings for the animation.

Viewport Navigational Controls

The **Viewport Navigation Controls** are located at the right end of the status bar [see Figure F52].

F52

The controls in the **Viewport Navigational Controls** depend on the type of viewport [Perspective, orthographic, camera, or light] active. Some of the buttons have a little black triangle at the right bottom corner. The arrow indicates that there are some hidden buttons exist. To view them, press and hold the LMB on the button. When a button is active, it is highlighted, to deactivate it, press **ESC**, choose another tool, or RMB click in a viewport.

Table 7 shows the controls available for all viewports. Table 8 shows the controls available for perspective and orthographic views. Table 9 shows the controls available for the camera views. Table 10 shows the controls available for the camera views.

Table 7: The viewport navigational controls available for all viewports		
Item	**Icon**	**Description**
Zoom Extents All, Zoom Extents All Selected		Allow you to zoom selected objects or all objects to their extent in the viewport.
Maximize Viewport Toggle		It switches any active viewport between its normal size and full-screen size. Hotkeys: **Alt+W**.

Table 8: The viewport navigational controls available for perspective and orthographic views		
Item	**Icon**	**Description**
Zoom		Allows you to change the magnification by dragging in a Perspective or orthographic viewport. Hotkeys: **Alt+Z**. You can also use the bracket keys, [and].
Zoom All		Allows you adjust view magnification in all Perspective and orthographic viewports at the same time.
Zoom Extents/Zoom Extents Selected		**Zoom Extents** centers all visible objects in an active Perspective or orthographic viewport until it fills the viewport. Hotkeys: **Ctrl+Alt+Z**. Zoom Extents Selected centers a selected object, or set of objects. Hotkey:**Z**.
Field-of-View Button (Perspective) or Zoom Region		**Field-of-View** adjusts the amount of the scene that is visible in a viewport. It's only available in the Perspective viewport. Hotkeys: **Ctrl+W. Zoom Region** magnifies a rectangular area you drag within a viewport.
Pan View		**Pan View** moves the view parallel to the current viewport plane. Hotkeys: **Ctrl+P**.
Walk Through		Allows you to move through a viewport by pressing arrow keys. Hotkey: **Up Arrow**.
Orbit, Orbit Selected, Orbit Sub-Object		**Orbit** rotates the viewport and uses the view center as the center of rotation. Hotkeys: **Ctrl+R. Orbit Selected** uses the center of the current selection as the center of rotation. **Orbit Sub-object** uses the center of the current sub-object selection as the center of rotation.

Table 9: The viewport navigational controls available for camera views

Item	Icon	Description
Dolly Camera, Target, or Both		This flyout replaces the **Zoom** button when the **Camera** viewport is active. Use these tools to move camera and/or its target along the camera main axis.
Perspective		It performs a combination of FOV and Dolly for target cameras and free cameras.
Roll Camera		Rotates a free camera around its local Z-axis.
Field-of-View Button		Adjusts the amount of the scene that is visible in a viewport
Truck Camera		Moves the camera parallel to the view plane.
Walk Through		Allows you move through a viewport by pressing a set of shortcut keys.
Orbit/Pan Camera		**Orbit Camera** rotates a camera about the target. **Pan Camera** rotates the target about the camera.

Table 10: The viewport navigational controls available for light views

Item	Icon	Description
Dolly Light, Target, or Both		Moves the light or its target or both along the light's main axis, toward or away from what the light is pointing at.
Light Hotspot		Allows you adjust the angle of a light's hotspot.
Roll Light		Roll Light rotates the light about its own line of sight (the light's local Z axis).
Light Falloff		Adjusts the angle of a light's falloff.
Truck Light		Moves a target light and its target parallel to the light view, and moves a free light in its XY plane.
Orbit/Pan Light		Rotates a light about the target. **Pan Light** rotates the target about the light.

Interaction Mode Preferences

If you are an **Autodesk Maya** user then it's good news for you that you can change the interaction mode to **Maya**. The **Interaction Mode** panel of the **Preferences** dialog box [see Figure F53] allows you to set the mouse and keyboard shortcut according to **3ds Max** or **Maya**.

When you set **Interaction Mode** to **Maya**, most of the shortcuts and mouse operations behave as they do in **Autodesk Maya**.

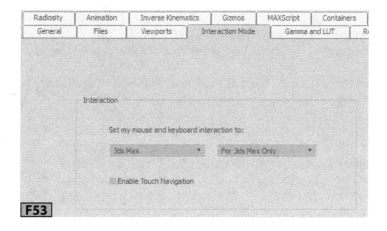

Here's the list:

- Pressing **Spacebar** maximizes the viewport that is beneath the mouse pointer.
- **Shift+Click** adds or removes from the selection. **Ctrl+Click** removes from the selection.
- The **Orbit** tools are not available in in the orthographic views.
- **Alt+Home** switches to the default perspective view.
- **Alt+LMB** drag to rotate the view. **Alt+MMB** drag to pan the view. **Alt+RMB** drag to zoom in or out in the view.

Table 11 shows a comparison between **3ds Max** and **Maya** hotkeys.

Table 11: The comparison between 3ds Max and Maya hotkeys		
Function	**3ds Max**	**Maya**
Maximize Viewport Toggle	Alt+W	Spacebar
Zoom Extents Selected	Z	F
Zoom Extents All	Shift+Ctrl+Z	A
Undo Viewport Operation	Shift+Z	Alt+Z
Redo Viewport Operation	Shift+Y	Alt+Y
Play Animation	/	Alt+V
Set Key	K	S
Group	None	Ctrl+G
Editable Poly Repeat Last Operation	;	G

Getting Around in 3ds Max

In the previous section, you have seen various components of the 3ds Max's UI. Don't get hung up on all the buttons, commands, menus, and options. It was a quick tour of the interface to get your feet wet. The more time you spent on **Unit MI1** and **Unit MI2**, easier it will be for you to understand rest of the units.

You can't do much with a blank scene. You need some objects in the scene in order to work on them. 3ds Max offers a wide range of standard objects. Let's start with creating some geometry in the scene.

Start 3ds Max, if not already running. Press **Alt+F+R** to open the 3ds Max message box. Click **Yes** to reset the scene.

Notice there are several panels in the **Command Panel: Create, Modify, Hierarchy, Motion, Display,** and **Utilities**. Position the mouse pointer on a panel's icon; a tooltip appears showing the name of the panel. The **Create** panel comprises of the following basic categories: **Geometry, Shapes, Lights, Cameras, Helpers, Space Warps,** and **Systems**. Each category is farther divided into sub-categories.

Notice in [see Figure F54] the **Create** panel [marked as 1], the **Geometry** button [marked as 2] is active. Below that button you will see a drop-down [marked as 3] that contains the **Geometry** sub-categories 3ds Max offers. Notice the **Standard Primitives** is selected by default in the drop-down.

Below the drop-down there is **Object Type** rollout [marked as 4]. There are ten buttons in this rollout. When you click on one of the buttons, the corresponding tool gets active and then you can create an object in the scene interactively using the mouse or by entering precise values using the keyboard.

Let's create an object from the **Standard Primitive** sub-category. Ensure you are in the **Command Panel | Create** panel **| Geometry** category **| Standard Primitives**. Now, click on **Box** in the **Object Type** rollout. Notice four rollouts appears in the **Create** panel: **Name and Color, Creation Method, Keyboard Entry,** and **Parameters**.

The **Keyboard Entry** rollout is collapsed whereas the other two are in the expanded state. Expand the **Keyboard Entry** rollout by clicking on the title bar of the rollout. Set **Length** to **50, Width** to **50,** and **Height** to **10**. Click **Create**. You need to press **Enter** or **Tab** after typing the values. Congratulations, you have created your first object in 3ds Max [see Figure F55].

You have not changed values of the **X, Y,** and **Z** controls in the **Keyboard Entry** rollout. As a result, the box is created at the origin of the home grid [0, 0, 0].

Also, notice the name of the object [**Box001**] in the **Name and Color** rollout. Every time you create an object in the scene, 3ds Max assigns it a default name. Collapse the **Keyboard Entry** rollout. On the **Parameters** rollout, change **Length** and **Width** to **100**.

Notice the box in the scene resizes as per the new dimensions you have set for the **Length** and **Width** controls. The change occurs because still **Box** is active in the **Object Type** rollout. If you select any other tool, then you would not be able to modify values from the **Create** panel.

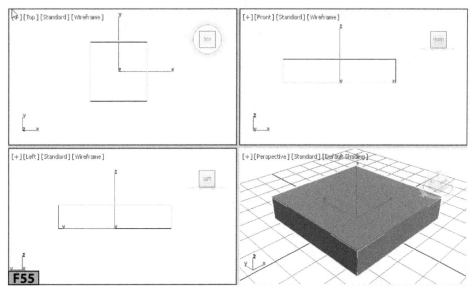

F55

Then, how to change the parameters? Well, once you select any other tool, you can change values for controls from the **Modify** panel [panel available on the right of the **Create** panel]. Click the **Modify** panel [see Figure F56] and notice the **Parameters** rollout appears there. Change **Height** to **20**.

F56

Change **Length Segs**, **Width Segs**, and **Height Segs** to **2** each. Notice the change is reflected on the object in the viewport.

Notice the white brackets around the box in the **Perspective** viewport. These are selection brackets that show the bounding box of the object. I am not a big fan of the selection brackets and don't find them very useful. Press **J** to get rid of the selection brackets. In order to change values for controls of an object from the **Parameters** rollout, the object must be selected in the viewport. I will cover selection methods later in the unit.

Click the **General Viewport** label in the **Perspective** viewport and choose **Configure Viewports** from the popup menu. In the **Viewport Configuration** dialog that appears, choose the **Layout** tab and then click on the layout button highlighted with white borders in Figure F57. Now, click **OK** to change the viewport layout [see Figure F58].

You have just changed the viewport layout. The **Top**, **Front**, and **Left** viewports are stacked over each other on the left and on the right you will see enlarged **Perspective** viewport. I frequently change viewport layout as per my needs. In this book, especially in hands-on exercises, if you find a different viewport layout in captures, this is the place from where you can change it. I have not written this process in hands-on exercises.

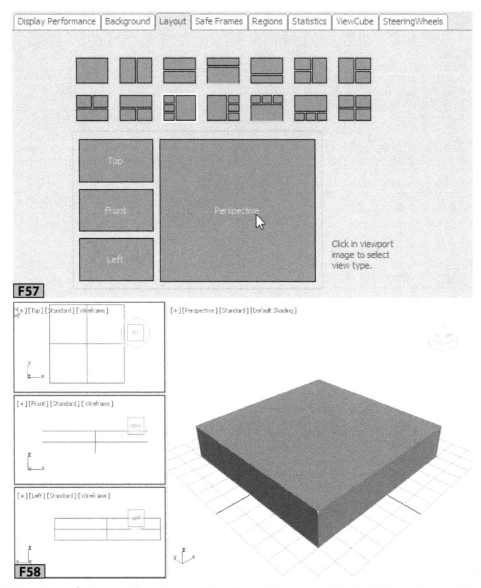

MMB click on the **Left** viewport to make it active. Press **B** to change it to the **Bottom** viewport. Press **L** to change it to the **Left** viewport. As discussed earlier, the options for changing the viewport are available in the **Point-Of-View [POV]** viewport label menu. Now onward, I will refer **Point-Of-View [POV]** viewport label menu as **POV** viewport label menu.

Notice the label for the **Shading Viewport** label reads **Realistic**. Click on the **Shading Viewport** label to display the **Shading Viewport** label menu. The options in this menu allow you to define the shading style for the viewport. The default shading style is **Realistic**. **Realistic** displays textures geometry realistically. Also, the shading and lighting in the viewport is of high quality. **Shaded** smoothly shades the geometry in the viewport using the **Phong** shader. **Facets** displays faceted geometry. It ignores the smooth group settings of the geometry.

MI1-34   Unit MI1: Introducing 3ds Max - I

Consistent Colors shows the raw color in the viewport ignoring lighting. **Edged Faces** shows the edges of the face. Figure F59 shows the teapot in **Realistic**, **Shaded**, **Facets**, **Consistent Colors**, and **Edged Faces** shading modes, respectively. The hotkeys for **Realistic** and **Edged** Face modes are **Shift+F3** and **F4**, respectively. You can toggle these modes using **Shift+F3** and **F4** hotkeys.

Hidden Line hides the faces and vertices whose normals are pointing away from the viewport. Shadows are unavailable in this mode. **Wireframe** displays objects in wireframe mode. The hotkey for toggling the **Wireframe** mode is **F3**. **Bounding Box** displays the edges of the bounding box of the geometry. **Clay** displays geometry in an uniform terracotta color. Figure F60 shows the teapot in the **Hidden Line**, **Wireframe**, **Bounding Box**, and **Clay** modes, respectively.

My favorite shading mode for modeling is **Clay** with **Edges Faces** and I have extensively used it in this book.

Press **Ctrl+S** to open the **Save File As** dialog and then type the name of the file in the **File name** text box and click **Save** to save the file. Now, if you want to open this file later, choose **Open** from the **Application** menu to open the **Open File** dialog. Navigate to the file and then click **Open** to open the file. If you want to save an already saved file with different name, choose **Save As** from the **Application** menu. You can also save a copy to the previous version of 3ds Max, choose **Save As** from the **Application** menu to open the **Save File As** dialog. In this dialog, choose the appropriate option from the **Save as type** drop-down [see Figure F61]. Click **Save** to save the file.

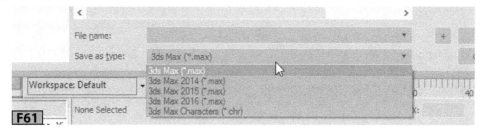

Tip: Incremental Save
*When you are working on a file, I highly recommend that you save different versions of it. If the current version gets corrupt, you can always fall back to a previous version of the file. 3ds Max allows you to save the file incrementally. In the **Save File As** dialog, click + on the left of **Save** to save the file with a name ending in a number greater than the current number displayed with the file name. For example, if the current name is **x1.max**, clicking + will save file with the name **x02.max**.*

Tip: Quick Access Toolbar
*You can also open and save files using the options available in the **Quick Access Toolbar**.*

Selecting Objects

Selecting objects is an important process before you perform any action on an object or objects. Selection in 3ds Max works on the noun-verb terminology. You first select the object (**the noun**) and then execute a command (**the verb**). 3ds Max provides a wide variety of tools for selecting objects. The **Selection** commands and functions are found in the following areas of interface:

- Main toolbar
- Edit menu
- Quad menu
- Tools menu
- Track View
- Display panel
- Modify panel
- Ribbon
- Schematic View
- Scene Explorer

Selecting Objects using Main toolbar Selection Buttons

The buttons available on the **Main** toolbar provides direct means of selection. These buttons are: **Select Object**, **Select by Name**, **Select and Move**, **Select and Rotate**, **Select and Scale**, and **Select and Manipulate**. To select an object, click on one of the selection buttons on the **Main** toolbar. Position the mouse pointer on the object that you want to select. The shape of the pointer changes to a small cross if the object is eligible for the selection. Click on the object to select it and de-select any selected object.

Note: Valid surface for selection
*The valid selection zone for the surface depends on the type of the object you are selecting and shading mode of the viewport in which you are selecting the object. In **Shaded** mode, any visible area of the surface is valid selection zone whereas in the **Wireframe** mode any edge or segment of the object is valid including the hidden lines.*

Adding and Removing Objects from the Current Selection

To extend a selection [adds objects to the existing selection], press and hold **Ctrl** while you make selections. For example, if you have selected two objects and you want to add third object to the selection, press and hold **Ctrl** and click on the third object to add it to the selection. To remove an object from selection, press and hold **Alt** and click on the object that you want to remove from the selection.

Inverting Selection

To invert the selection, choose **Select Invert** from the **Edit** menu. The hotkeys for this operation are **Ctrl+I**. For example, if you have total five objects in the scene and three of them are selected. Now, to select the remaining two objects and terminating the current selection, press **Ctrl+I**.

Selecting All Objects

To select all objects, choose **Select All** from the **Edit** menu or press **Ctrl+A**.

Locking the Selection

When the selection is locked, you can click-drag mouse anywhere in the viewport without losing the selection. To lock a selection, click **Selection Lock Toggle** [see Figure F62] from the **Status Bar** or press **Spacebar**. Press **Spacebar** again to unlock the selection.

Deselecting an Object

To deselect an object, click on another object, or click on an empty area of the viewport. To deselect all objects in a scene, choose **Select None** from the **Edit** menu.

Selecting by Region

The region selection tools in 3ds Max allow you to select one more object by defining a selection region using mouse. By default, a rectangular region is created when you drag the mouse. You can change the region by picking a region type from the **Region** flyout [see Figure F63] **Main** toolbar.

Note: Using Ctrl and Alt

*If you draw a selection region with the **Ctrl** held down, the affected objects are added to the selection. Conversely, if you hold down **Alt**, the affected objects are removed from the selection.*

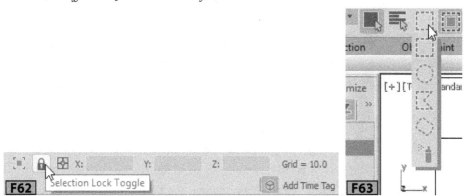

Table 12 lists the types of region selection. Figure F61 shows the rectangular, circular, fence, lasso, and paint marquee selections, respectively.

Table 12: The region selection types	
Type	**Description**
Rectangular	Allows you select objects using the rectangular selection region.
Circular	Allows you select objects using the circular selection region.
Fence	Allows you to draw an irregular selection region.
Lasso	Allows you to draw an irregular selection region with single mouse operation.
Paint	Activates a brush. Paint on the objects to add them to the selection.

Note: Changing the Brush Size

*You can change the brush size from the **Preferences** dialog. RMB on the **Paint Selection** type to open the dialog. In the **General** panel | **Scene Selection** area, you can set the brush size by specifying a value for the **Paint Selection Brush Size** control. The default value for this control is **20**.*

The button on the right of the **Region Selection** flyout is a toggle button. It allows you to specify whether to include objects touched by the region border. This button affects all region selection methods I have described above. The default state of the button is **Crossing**. It selects all objects that are within the region and crossing the boundary of the region [see Figure F65]. The other state of the button is **Window**. It selects only those objects that are completely within the region [see Figure F66].

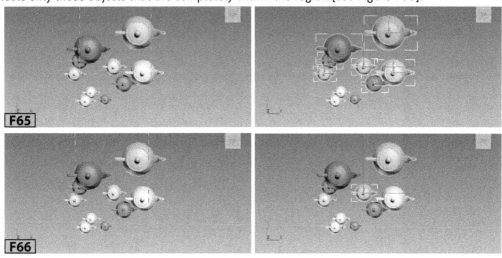

Select By Name

On clicking the **Select By Name** button on the **Main** toolbar, the **Select From Scene** dialog appears [see Figure F67]. It allows you to select objects by their assigned names.

To select objects by name, click **Select By Name** on the **Main** toolbar or press **H** to open the **Select From Scene** dialog. It lists all the objects in the scene. Click on the names of one or more objects to select them and then click **OK** to select the object and close the dialog and select the highlighted objects. Use **Ctrl+click** to highlight more than one entry in this dialog.

Tip: Quickly selecting an object
*To select a single object, double-click on its name to select it and close the **Select By Name** dialog.*

Named Selection Sets

You can name a selection in 3ds Max and then recall the selection by choosing their name from a list. To assign a name to the selection, select one or more objects or sub-objects in the scene. Click on the **Named Selection** field [see Figure F68] on the **Main** toolbar to activate a text box and then type a name for your selection set. Press **Enter** to complete the operation.

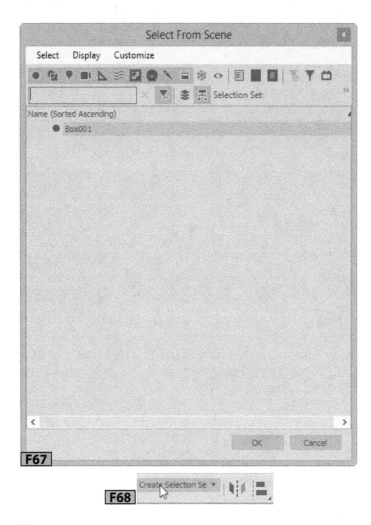

F67

F68

Caution: Case sensitive names
The names you enter for the selection are case-sensitive.

To retrieve a named selection set, click the **Named Selection Sets** list's arrow. Choose the desired name from the list. The corresponding objects are selected in the viewport. You can also select the selection sets from the **Named Selection Sets** dialog [see Figure F69]. To open this dialog, click **Edit Named Selection Sets** from the **Main** toolbar. Highlight the name of the set in this dialog and then click **Select Objects in Set** from the **Named Selection Sets** dialog's toolbar.

Using the Selection Filters

You can use the **Selection Filter** list [see Figure F70] to deactivate selection of all but a specific category by choosing category from this list. For example, if you select **Lights** from this list, you would be only select the light objects in the scene. To remove filtering, select **All** from this list.

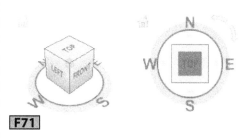

Using the Navigation Controls

3ds Max provides two controls to navigate a viewport: **ViewCube** and **SteeringWheels**. These semitransparent controls appear on the upper right corner of a viewport and allow you to change the view without using any menu, command, or keyboard.

ViewCube

This gizmo [see Figure F71] provides a visual feedback to you about the orientation of the viewport. It also lets you quickly switch between the standard and orthographic views. The **ViewCube** does not appear in the camera, light, or shape viewport as well as in the special type of views such as **ActiveShade** or **Schematic**. When the **ViewCube** is inactive, the primary function of the **ViewCube** is to show the orientation of the model based on the north direction of the model. The inactive **ViewCube** remains in the semi-transparent state. When you position the mouse pointer on it, it becomes active.

Tip: Toggling the visibility of the ViewCube
*Press **Ctrl+Alt+V** to toggle the **ViewCube's** visibility.*

If you hover the mouse pointer on top of the **ViewCube**, you will notice that faces, edges, and corners of the cube are highlighted. Click on the highlighted part of the cube; 3ds Max animates the viewport and orients it according to the clicked part of the cube. Click on the home icon on the **ViewCube** to switch to the default viewport orientation. You can also click and drag the ring to spin model around its current orientation.

To change the **ViewCube's** settings, RMB click on the **ViewCube** and choose **Configure** from the popup menu to open the **Viewport Configuration** dialog [see Figure F72] with the **ViewCube** panel active. From this panel you can change various settings for the **ViewCube**.

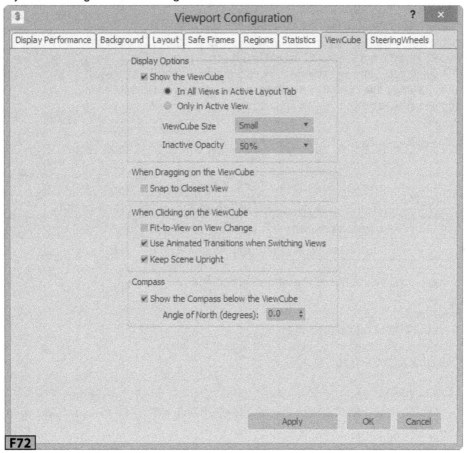

F72

Table 13 lists the other option available in the popup menu.

Table 13: The options available for **ViewCube** in the popup menu

Option	Description
Home	Restores the home view.
Orthographic	Changes the current orientation to the orthographic projection.
Perspective	Changes the current orientation to the perspective projection.
Set Current View as Home	Defines the home view based on the current orientation.
Set Current View as Front	Defines the front projection based on the current projection.
Reset Front	Resets the front projection to its default view.
Configure	Opens the **Viewport Configuration** dialog.

| Help | Launches the online help system and navigate to the **ViewCube's** documentation. |

SteeringWheels

The **SteeringWheels** gizmo [see Figure F73] allows you to access different 2D and 3D navigation tools from a single tool. When you first start 3ds max, the **SteeringWheels** gizmo is not available. To enable this gizmo press **Shift+W**. When the wheel is displayed, you can activate it by clicking on one of its wedges. If you click drag a wedge, the current view changes. The navigation tools listed in Table 14 support click action.

F73

Table 14: The navigation tools	
Tool	**Function**
Zoom	Adjust the magnification of the view.
Center	Centers the view based on the position of the mouse pointer.
Rewind	Restores the previous view.
Forward	Increases the magnification of the view.

To close a wheel, you can use one of the following methods:

1. Press **Esc**.
2. Press **Shift+W** to toggle the wheel.
3. Click the small **x** button the upper right area of the wheel.
4. RMB click on the wheel.

Tip: Changing wheel's settings
*You can change the **SteeringWheels'** settings from the **SteeringWheels** panel of the **Viewport Configuration** dialog box [see Figure F74].*

There are other versions of the wheels available that you can activate from the **Wheel** menu. To open the menu, click on the down arrow on the bottom-right corner of the wheel. Table 15 lists those options.

Table 15: The options available in the **Wheel** menu.	
Option	**Function**
Mini View Object Wheel	Displays the mini version of the **View Object** wheel [see the first image in Figure F75].
Mini Tour Building Wheel	Displays the mini version of the **Tour Building** wheel [see the second image in Figure F75].
Mini Full Navigation Wheel	Displays the mini version of the **Full Navigation** wheel [see the third image in Figure F75].
Full Navigation Wheel	Displays the big version of the **Full Navigation** wheel [see the fourth image in Figure F75].

Basic Wheels	Displays the big versions of the **View Object** or **Tour Building** wheel [Figure F76].
Go Home	Restores the **Home** view.
Restore Original Center	Pans the view to the origin.
Increase Walk Speed	Doubles the walk speed used by the **Walk** tool.
Decrease Walk Speed	Cuts the walk speed by half used by the **Walk** tool.
Help	Navigates you to the online documentation of the steering wheels.
Configure	Opens the **Viewport Configuration** dialog that allows you set preferences for the wheel.

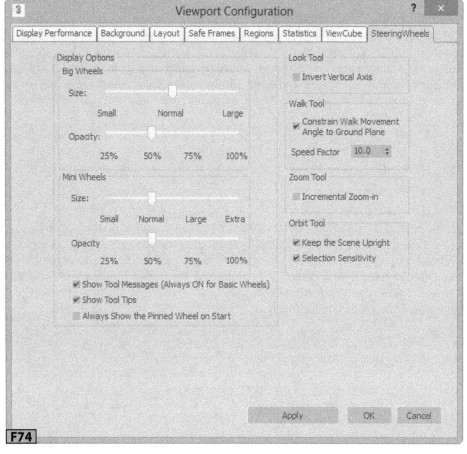

F74

F75

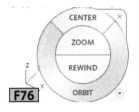
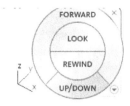

Zooming, Panning, and Orbiting Views using Mouse Scroll

To zoom in and out in the viewport, scroll the mouse wheel. It zooms in or out in steps and is equivalent to using bracket keys, **[** and **]**. If you want to gradually zoom, scroll the wheel with the **Ctrl+Alt** held down. Press and hold MMB and then drag the mouse pointer to pan the view. You can pan the viewport in any direction. To rotate the viewport press and hold **Alt+MMB** and then drag the mouse pointer.

Moving, Rotating, and Scaling Objects

The transformation tools [see Figure F77] in 3ds Max allow you to move, rotate, and scale an object[s]. A transformation is the adjustment position, orientation, and scale relative to the 3D space you are working in. 3ds Max provides four tools that allow you to transform the object: **Select and Move**, **Select and Rotate**, **Select and Scale**, and **Select and Place**. The **Select and Move**, **Select and Rotate**, and **Select and Scale** tools are generally referred as **Move**, **Rotate**, and **Scale** tools. Now onward, I will use these names.

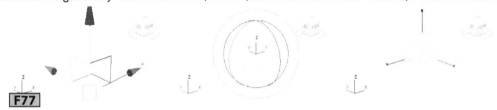

To transform an object, click the **Move**, **Rotate**, or **Scale** button from the **Main** toolbar. Position the mouse pointer on the object[s]. If the object[s] is already selected, the shape of the cursor changes to indicate transform. If object[s] is not selected, the shape of the mouse pointer changes to a crosshair. Now, drag the mouse pointer to apply the transform. You can restrict the motion to one or two axes by using the transform gizmos. The transform gizmos are the icons displayed in the viewport. Figure F77 shows the **Move**, **Rotate**, and **Scale** gizmos, respectively.

Tip: Changing size of the gizmos
You can change the size of the gizmos by using the – and = keys on the main keyboard.

When no transform tool is active and you select objects, an axis tripod appears in the viewports [see Figure F78]. Each axis tripod consists of three lines labeled as **X**, **Y**, and **Z**. The orientation of the tripod indicates the orientation of the current reference coordinate system.

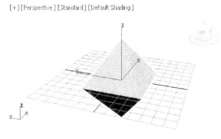

The point where the three lines meet indicates the current transform center and the highlighted red axis lines show the current axis constraints.

Each gizmo indicates axes by using three colors: **X** is **red**, **Y** is **green**, and **Z** is **blue**. You can use any of the axes handles to constrain transformation to that axis.

Tip: 1-minute learning movies
To more about transform tools, download the movies from the following link: http://download.autodesk.com/us/3dsmax/ skillmovies/index.html.

The transform commands are also available from the **Quad** menu. To transform an object using the **Quad** menu, RMB click on the selected object[s], choose the transform command from the **Quad** menu and then drag the object to apply the transform.

Tip: Cancelling transform
To cancel a transform, RMB click while dragging the mouse.

Using the Transform Type-In dialog
You can use the **Transform Type-In** dialog to precisely enter the transformation values. To transform objects using this dialog, if the **Move**, **Rotate**, or **Scale** tool is active, press **F12** to open the dialog or choose **Transform Type-In** from the **Edit** menu to open the associated **Transform Type-In** dialog. Figure F79 shows the **Move Transform Type-In**, **Rotate Transform Type-In**, and **Scale Transform Type-In** dialogs, respectively. You can enter both the absolute and relative transformation values in this dialog.

Tip: Transform Type-In dialog
*You can also open this dialog by RMB clicking on the tool's button on the **Main** toolbar.*

The controls in this dialog are also replicated in the **Status Bar**. You can use these **Transform Type-In** boxes on the **Status Bar** to transform the object. To switch between the absolute and relative transform modes, click the **Relative/Absolute Transform Type-In** button on the **Status Bar** [see Figure F80].

Getting Help

Autodesk provides rock solid documentation for 3ds Max. There are several places in the UI from where you can access different forms of help. The help options are listed in the **Help** menu [see Figure F81]. Click **Autodesk 3ds Max Help** from the **Help** menu to open the online documentation for 3ds Max. You can also download offline help from the Autodesk website and install on your computer. If you have a slow internet connection, you can download the offline help and use it. To access offline help, download and install it on your system. Press **Alt+U+P** hotkeys to open the **Preferences** dialog [refer Figure F82].

Choose the **Help** panel from the dialog and click **Browse** to open the **Browser For Folder** dialog. In this dialog, navigate to the directory where you installed help, generally, *C:\Program Files (x86)\Autodesk\ Help\3dsmax2017\en_us*. Click **OK** to close the dialog. Click **OK** from the **Preferences** dialog to close it. Now, when you press **F1**, 3ds Max will navigate you to the offline help.

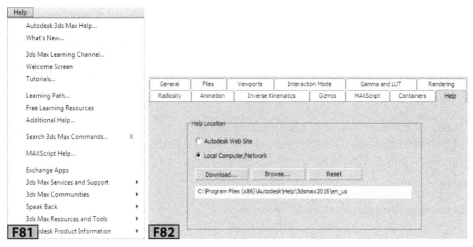

F81 F82

Search Command

The search command feature was introduced in 2014 version of 3ds Max. This feature helps you finding a specific command. For example, if you are looking for the **Sunlight** tool but not sure where it is on the interface. Press **X** to open the **Search Command** text box and then type **Sun; SunLight** System appears in a list [see Figure F83]. Click on it, 3ds Max takes you to **Systems** category of the **Create** panel in the **Command Panel**.

InfoCenter Toolbar

The **InfoCenter** is located on the right of caption bar at the top-right of the UI [see Figure F84]. This toolbar allows you to access information about 3ds Max as well as other Autodesk products.

F83 F84

Table 16 shows the elements of this toolbar.

Table 16: The **InfoCenter** toolbar interface overview		
Element	**Icon**	**Description**
Search field	-	The search box is marked by arrow in Figure F81. You can use this search box to lookup information in the help documentation. This field supports wildcard characters such as * and ?.
Communication Center		Takes you to the **Communication Center** that displays announcements about product updates and other news.
Favorites		Click to view the **Favorite** panel.

Sign In		Allows you to access Autodesk 360 for mobility, collaboration, and online services of the cloud.
Autodesk Exchange Apps		Takes you to the Autodesk Exchange Application store.
Quick Help menu		Takes you to quick help menu which is a smaller version of the **Help** menu.

Hands-on Exercise

Before you start the exercise, let's first create a project folder for the hands-on exercise of this unit. You can proceed without creating a project folder but I highly recommend that you create one. The project folder allows you to keep your file organized.

Open the **Windows Explorer** and create a new directory with the name **max2017projects** in the **C** drive of your system. Start 3ds Max. From the **Application** menu, choose **Reset**. Click **Yes** from the dialog that opens.

From the **Application** menu, choose **Manage | Set Project Folder** to open the **Browse for Folder** dialog. Navigate to the **3dsmax2017projects** directory and then click **Make New Folder**. Create the new folder with the name **unit-mi1** and click **OK** to create the project directory.

Now, if you navigate to the **\max2017projects\unit-mi1** directory, you will see a number of sub-directories [see Figure E1].

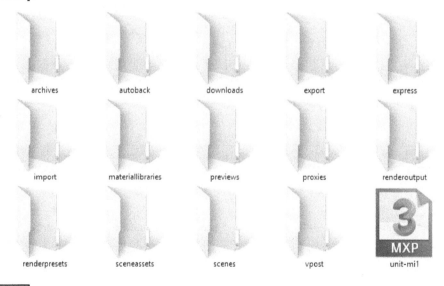

E1

What just happened?
Here, I have set a project folder for the hands-on exercise of this unit. When you set a project folder for a scene, 3ds Max creates a series of folders such as **scenes**, **sceneassets**, *and so forth. These folders are default locations for certain types of operations in 3ds Max. For example, the* **scenes** *folder is used when 3ds Max opens or saves scene files.*

*It is a good idea to reset the scene before you start new work because the **Open** command defaults to the folder where the previous scene was saved. After the reset operation, the **Open** command defaults to the **scenes** folder of the current project folder.*

The **unit-mi1** folder will contain all the data related to the hands-on exercise of this unit.

Exercise 1: Creating Simple Model of a House

OK, now it is time to work on the first exercise of the book. In this exercise, you will create a simple model of a house using the **Standard Primitives** [see Figure E2].

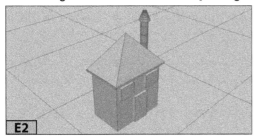 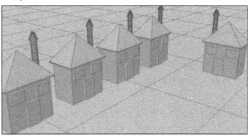

Table E1 summarizes the exercise:

Table E1 - Creating a Simple Model of a House	
In this exercise, you will learn how to	• Reset 3ds Max settings • Create objects • Use navigational controls • Align objects • Undo and redo scene views • Use navigational gizmos • Use **Transform Type-In** boxes
Skill level	Beginner
Project Folder	**unit-mi1**
Time to complete	20 Minutes
Final exercise file	**umi1-hoe1-end.max**

Start 3ds Max. Choose **Reset** from the **Application** menu or press **Alt+F+R**. Click **Yes** on the **3ds Max** message box to reset the settings. Choose **Unit Setup** from the **Customize** menu to open the **Units Setup** dialog. Ensure that **Generic Units** in on in this dialog box and then click **OK** to close the dialog.

Click **Box** on the **Object Type** rollout in the **Command Panel** and then click-drag in the **Perspective** viewport to define the length and width of the box. Release the mouse button to define the length and width of the box. Release the LMB and then drag upward to define the height. Click to specify the height.

Press **J** to turn off the selection brackets and **F4** to turn on the **Edged Faces** mode. Now, click on the **Shading Viewport** label and choose **Clay** from the popup menu. Press **G** To turn off the grid. Press **G** again to turn it on. Drag the mouse pointer with the **MMB+Alt** held down to rotate the view. Drag the mouse pointer with the **MMB** held down to pan the view. Drag the mouse pointer with the **Ctrl+Alt+MMB** held down to zoom in or out of the view. You need to place the mouse pointer on the area for which you want to change the magnification.

Next, you will use the brackets keys to change the settings.

Place the mouse pointer on the area for which you want to change the magnification settings and then use the bracket keys **[** and **]** to change the level of magnification. MMB click on the **Perspective** viewport to make it active, if not already active. Press **Alt+W** to maximize the viewport. Click on the **Home** icon on the **ViewCube** to restore the home view. Alternatively, you can RMB click on the **ViewCube** and then choose **Home** from the **ViewCube's** menu. Press **Alt+W** again to restore the four viewport arrangement. Click drag the compass ring of the **ViewCube** to change the orientation of the viewport. Now, click-drag edges, corners, or faces of the **ViewCube** and experiment with various possibilities that **ViewCube** offers. When done, click on the **Home** icon to restore the view.

Press **Shift+Z** repeatedly to undo the scene view changes. Press **Shift+Y** to redo the scene view changes. Click on the **ViewCube's Home** icon to restore the home view. Press **Ctrl+P** to activate the **Pan View** 🖐 tool and then drag in the viewport to pan the view. Now, press **Ctr+R** to activate the **Orbit** tool and drag in the viewport to rotate the view. Press **Q** to deactivate the **Orbit** tool 🔄 and activate the **Select** tool. Press **Shift+W** to activate **StreeringWheels**. Click drag the **ZOOM** wedge to change the magnification level. Similarly, experiment with other wedges of the wheel. Press **Esc** to deactivate **SteeringWheels**.

Make sure **Box001** is selected in the viewport and then RMB click on the **Move** ✛ tool to open the **Move Transform Type-In** dialog. In the **Absolute:World** group of the dialog, RMB click on the spinners to set them to their default values which is **zero**. You will notice that the box is now placed at the origin in the viewports. The **Move Transform Type-In** dialog is a **modeless** dialog. You don't have to close it in order to work on the model we are creating in this exercise. Choose the **Modify** panel 🖉 in the **Command Panel**. In the **Parameters** rollout, set **Length**, **Width**, and **Height** to **80**, **50**, and **70**, respectively, to change the size of the box. Press **Ctrl+Shift+Z** to zoom the box to its extents in all viewports [see Figure E3].

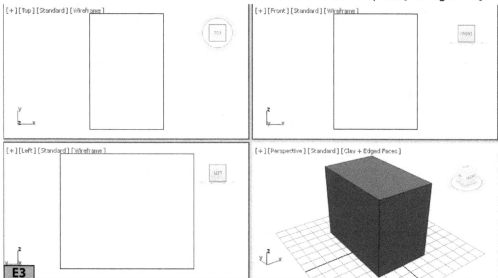

If you press **Z** the box will be zoomed in the active viewport only. Now, let's create door and windows of the house. Create another box in the **Perspective** viewport and then set its **Length**, **Width**, and **Height** to **23**, **6**, and **40**, respectively [see Figure E4]. Ensure **Box002** and the **Move** tool selected and then enter **-25**, **-2.3**, and **-0.03** in the **Transform Type-In** boxes in the **Status Bar** [see Figure E5].

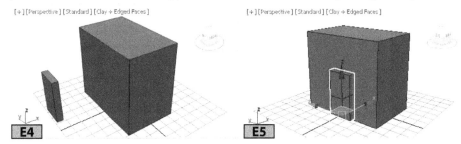

Create two windows using the **Box** primitive. Use the values **23**, **6**, and **18** for the **Length**, **Width**, and **Height** spinners, respectively. Now, align the boxes [see Figure E6]. Ensure the **Box** tool is active and then turn on **AutoGrid** from the **Object Type** rollout. Position the mouse pointer on the **Box001**, an axis tripod shows up [see Figure E7]. Create a box on the **Box001**.

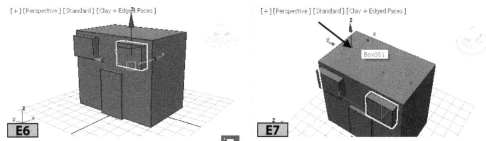

Ensure **Box005** is selected and then click **Align** on the **Main** toolbar. Now, click **Box001** in the **Perspective** viewport to open the **Align Selection** dialog. In this dialog, set the values as shown in Figure E8 and click **OK** to align the boxes.

Ensure **Box005** is selected and then choose the **Modify** panel. On the **Parameters** rollout, set **Length**, **Width**, and **Height** to **91**, **60**, and **2**, respectively [see Figure E9]. Choose the **Create** panel and ensure **Auto Grid** is on. Click **Pyramid** on the **Object Type** rollout and then create a pyramid on **Box005**. Align **Pyramid001** with **Box005**. Ensure **Pyramid001** is selected and then in the **Modify panel | Parameters** rollout, set **Width**, **Depth**, and **Height** to **60**, **90**, and **46**, respectively [see Figure E10].

Now, let's create a chimney for the house.

On the **Create** panel, choose **Cylinder** from the **Object Type** rollout and create a cylinder in the **Perspective** viewport. In the **Modify panel | Parameters** rollout, set **Radius** and **Height** to **5** and **60**, respectively. Now, place **Cylinder001** on the roof using the **Move** tool [see Figure E11]. In the **Create** panel, choose **Cone** from the **Object Type** rollout and ensure **AutoGrid** is on. Create a cone on **Cylinder001**. Align **Cone001** and **Cylinder001**.

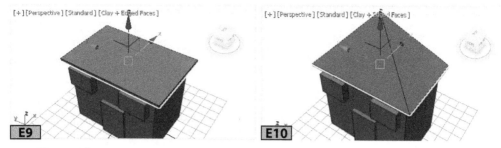

In the **Modify panel | Parameters** rollout, set **Radius 1**, **Radius 2**, and **Height** to **7.5**, **2**, and **13**, respectively [see Figure E12].

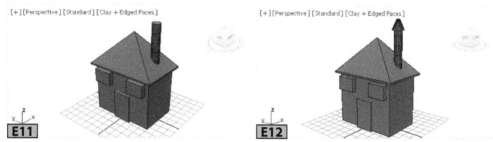

Choose **Select All** from the **Edit** menu to select all objects in the scene. Choose **Group** from the **Group** menu to open the **Group** dialog. In this dialog, type **House** in the **Group name** field and click **OK** to create a group. Press **Ctrl+S** to open the **Save File As** dialog. In this dialog, navigate to the location where you want to save the file. Type the name of the file in the **File name** text box and then click **Save** to save the file.

Practical Tests
Complete the following tests:

Test 1: Creating Text
Create the text [Love] as shown in Figure P1 using the **Box** primitive.

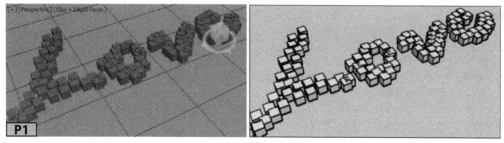

Test 2: Creating a Road Side Sign
Create a road side sign, as shown in Figure P2, using the **Box**, **Pyramid**, and **Box** primitives.

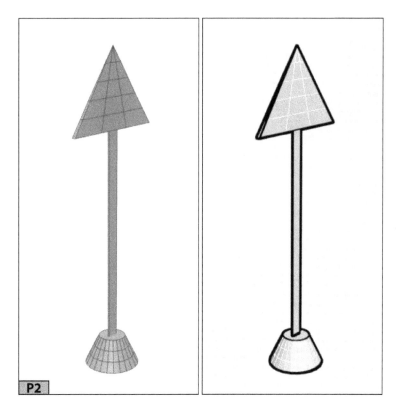

Explore More

Per-view Preferences and Presets

We can define display quality settings for each viewport. For example, you can specify the rendering level [**Basic**, **Advanced**, and **DX**], Lighting and Shadow settings, ambient occlusion settings, and so forth. The Per-view Preferences and Presets can be accessed from the **Viewport Setting and Preference** dialog [see Figure EM1]. To open this dialog, choose **Per-View Preset** from the third viewport label menu or **Per-View Preference** from the fourth viewport label menu.

Creative Market Store

You can buy 3D assets from independent creators using the **Autodesk Creative Market Store**. To open the store, choose **Creative Market Store** from the **Content** menu to open the **Creative Market** in-application browser. You need to have an account with the store before you start using it. This store is same as their website which is available at the following address: *https://creativemarket.com/3d*.

Asset Library Application

You can download the application from the Autodesk site and the use it to navigate and download files from **Autodesk seek**. It allows you to quickly access 3D content on your local computer and network in a single view, making all content instantly searchable. You can also drag and drop scenes from your local hard drive. Once installed, you can launch the application from the Window **Start** menu or you can choose Launch **3ds Max Asset Library** from the **Content** menu. After you zero-in on a desired asset, you can control how the asset will integrate with scene through Xref, merge or replace.

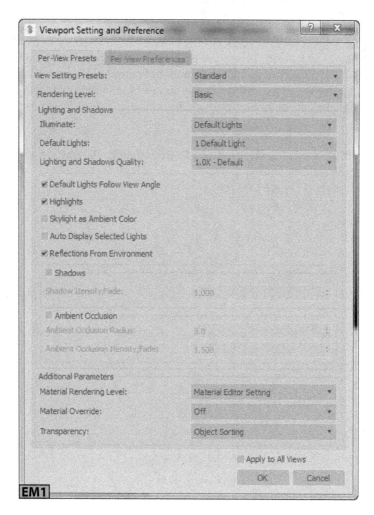

EM1

Sending Files to Print Studio

3ds Max allows you to send your 3D models to **Print Studio** which is a program for 3D printing. To access this feature, choose the **Application** button and then choose **Send to** | **Send to Print Studio** [see Figure EM2].

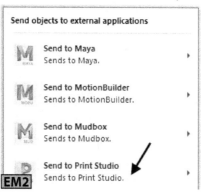

EM2

Game Exporter Utility

This utility [see Figure EM3] allows you to export the models and animations clips in **FBX** format to your game engine in a streamlined fashion. This utility is specifically designed for game users to export game assets more efficiently. This utility uses minimal amount of settings, as a result, you can easily export the model without changing too many settings. It also supports animation clips thus allows you to export multiple clips as a single FBX file or as multiple files. You can open this utility from the **Application** menu or **Utilities** panel:

- **Utilities** panel | **Utilities** rollout | **More** button | **Utilities** dialog | **Parameters** rollout | **Game Exporter** button
- **Application** menu | **Export** | **Game Exporter**

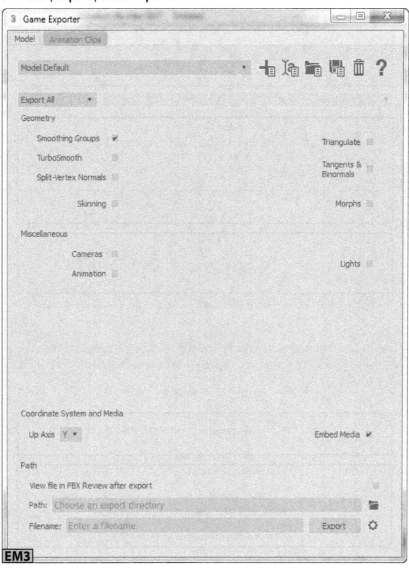

Summary

The unit covered the following topics:

- Understanding workspaces
- Navigating the workspace
- Customizing the interface
- Understanding various UI components
- Working with the file management commands
- Setting preferences for 3ds Max
- Understanding the enhanced menu system
- Working with viewports
- Setting preferences for the viewports
- Creating objects in the scene
- Selecting objects
- Using the navigational gizmos
- Moving, rotating, and scaling objects
- Getting help
- Per-view Preferences, Creative Market Store, Asset Library, Print Studio, and Game Exporter

This page intentionally left blank

Unit MI2: Introducing 3ds Max - II

In the previous unit, I covered the interface as well as the tools that allow you to transform objects in the viewport. In this unit, I will cover the tools and procedures that will help you immensely during the modeling process. You will know about various explorers as well as various precision tools that 3ds Max offers. I have also covered the procedures for creating clones, and duplicates.

In this unit, I will cover the following:

- Working with templates
- Creating clones and duplicates
- Understanding hierarchies
- Working with the **Scene** and **Layer** Explorers
- Understanding the **Mirror**, **Select and Place**, and **Select and Manipulate** tools
- Working with the **Align** and **Array** tools
- Working with precision and drawing aids
- Understanding modifiers, and normals

Working with Templates

Templates, introduced in 2016 version of 3ds Max allow you to create a base file that you can use to create new files based on a template. For example, if you regularly work on projects that consist of studio lighting, you can create a template with three point light setup, **mental ray** renderer, and HD resolution for rendering. The template will save you lot of time when you start working on a new project. The following information can be saved in templates:

- Scene and display units
- Renderer and rendering resolution
- Scene geometry, which can be animated
- The active workspace
- The order of rollouts
- The **ViewCube** settings
- Viewport layout and settings
- User paths

The start-up templates are available in the **Start** panel of the **Welcome Screen**. If the **Welcome Screen** is not visible, choose **Welcome Screen** from the **Help** menu. 3ds Max comes with some default templates that you can access from the **START-UP TEMPLATES** section of the **Start** panel. To start a new scene using a default template, double-click on a template preview. You can use a template by first selecting the preview icon and then clicking **New Using Selected Template**.

Click **Open Template Manager** from the **Start** panel of the **Welcome Screen** to open the **Template Manager** dialog [see Figure F1]. At the left of the dialog, you will see the preview icons of the available templates. Place the mouse pointer on the icons to view the brief description of the template. Click on an icon to see its details at the right of the dialog. Click **Set as Default** to make the selected template default for the new scenes. The array of buttons available for **Thumbnail** control allows you to set a preview icon for the template. The controls to set scene file, project folder, and workspace are available below these buttons.

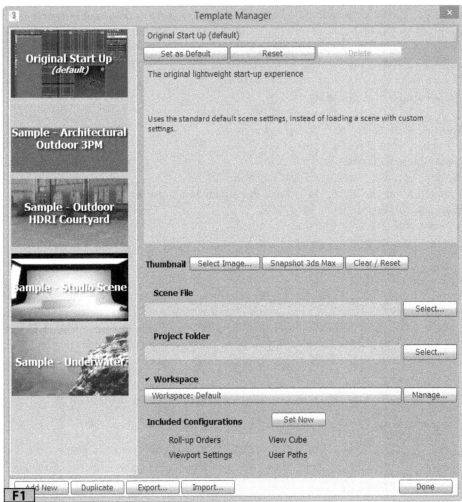

F1

To create a new template, click **Add New** and then provide the required information at the right of the dialog. Click **Done** to create a new template and close the **Template Manager** dialog. To duplicate an existing template, select the template and then click **Duplicate**.

Creating Copies, Clones, and References

The general terms used for duplicating objects is **cloning**. To create a duplicate, clone, or reference, transform [move, rotate, or scale] the object with **Shift** held down. This process is generally called

Shift+Transform. There are some other tools such as the **Mirror** tool available in 3ds Max that allows you to create clones.

Q: What's is the difference between Copy, Instance, and Reference?

*There are three methods available in 3ds Max to clone the objects: **Copy**, **Instance**, and **Reference**. At geometry level, clones created using any method are identical. However, they behave differently when used with the modifiers such as **Bend** or **Twist**.*

*The **Copy** method allows you to create a completely different copy of the original object. If you modify the original object, it will have no effect on the other. The **Instance** method creates a completely interchangeable clone of the original. If you modify the original or the instance, the change will be replicated in both objects. The **Reference** method creates a clone dependent on the original upto the point when the object was created. If you apply a new modifier to the referenced object, it will affect only that object. Depending on the method used, the cloned objects are called copies, instances, or references.*

Cloning Techniques

3ds Max provides several techniques for creating clones. You can use any of these techniques on any selection. Here's the list:

- Clone
- Shift+Clone
- Snapshot
- **Array** tool
- **Mirror** tool
- **Spacing** tool
- **Clone and Align** tool
- Copy/Paste (**Scene Explorer**)

Table 1 summarizes these techniques:

Table 1: The list of cloning techniques	
Technique	**Description**
Clone	The easiest method for creating clones is to use the **Clone** command. To create clone using this command, select the object[s] that you want to clone and then choose **Clone** from the **Edit** menu or press **Ctrl+V**. The **Clone Options** dialog appears. Choose the method you want to use from the **Object** section of the dialog and then specify a name for the cloned object using **Name** text box and then click **OK** to create a clone. The clone will be superimposed on the original object at the same location. Use the **Move** tool to separate the two.
Shift+Drag	You can use this technique to clone objects while transforming them. This technique is most used technique for cloning objects. To clone and transform objects, click **Move**, **Rotate**, or **Scale** on the **Main** toolbar and then select an object, multiple objects, group, or sub-objects in a viewport. Hold down **Shift** and then drag the selection. As you drag the selection the clone is created, and transformed. Now, release **Shift** and mouse button to open the **Clone Options** dialog. Change the settings and click **OK** to create a clone.

Snapshot	You can use this feature to create an animated object over time. You can create a single clone on any frame or you can create clones on multiple frames along the animation path. The spacing between the clones is a uniform time interval.
Array	You can use the **Array** tool to create repeating design patterns for example, legs of a round coffee table, blades of a jet engine, text on the dial of a watch, and so forth. The **Array** command allows you to precisely control the transformations in 3D space.
Mirror	**Mirror** allows you to create a symmetrical copy along any combination of axes. This tool also provide an option "**No Clone**" that allows you to perform a mirror operation without creating clone.
Spacing Tool	This tool distributes objects along a path define by a spline. You can control the spacing between the objects.
Clone and Align Tool	This tool allows you to distribute the source objects to a selection of the destination objects. This tool is very useful when you work on an imported CAD file that contains lots of symbols. For example, you can replace the chair symbols in the CAD file with the actual chair geometry en masse.
Copy/Paste (Scene Explorer)	You can use the **Scene Explorer's Edit** menu command to copy paste nodes. The **Scene Explorer** should be in **Sort By Hierarchy** mode.

Working with the Mirror Tool

On clicking **Mirror** from the **Main** toolbar, the **Mirror** dialog appears [see Figure F2]. The controls in this dialog allow you to mirror the current selection about the center of the current coordinate system. You can also create a clone while mirroring a selection. To mirror an object, make a selection in a viewport. Click **Mirror** on the **Main** toolbar or choose **Mirror** from the **Tools** menu. In the **Mirror** dialog that appears, set the parameters and click **OK** [see Figure F3]. In Figure F3, I have selected the left leg of the robot and then used the **Mirror** dialog to create his right leg.

Notice in the **Mirror** dialog, there are two options at the top: **Transform** and **Geometry**. These options control how the **Mirror** tool treats the reflected geometry. **Transform** uses the legacy mirror method. This method mirrors any word-space-modifiers [**WSM**] effect. **Geometry** applies a **Mirror** modifier to the object and does not mirror any **WSM** effect.

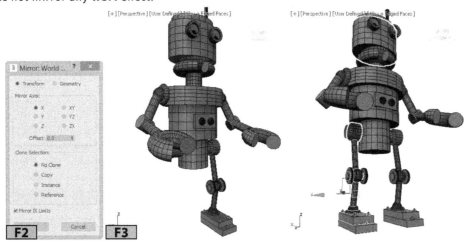

F2

F3

Tip: Mirrored arrays
You can create mirrored arrays using the **Mirror** and **Array** tools in succession.

Tip: Animating mirror operation
To animate the mirror operation, turn on **Auto Key** and then set a target frame for the transition to end. Now, mirror the object using the **Mirror** tool. The object will appear flatten and then reshape itself during the transition.

Tip: Coordinate System
The title bar of the **Mirror** dialog shows the current coordinate system in use.

Working with the Array Tool

The **Array** tool allows you to create an array of objects based on the current selection in the viewport. The **Array** button in not visible on the **Main** toolbar by default. The **Array** button is part of the **Extras** toolbar which is not visible by default. To make it visible, RMB click on a gray area of the **Main** toolbar and then choose **Extras** from the popup menu to display the **Extras** toolbar [see Figure F4].

Tip: Array command
The **Array** command is also available in the **Tools** menu.

Tip: Real-time update
Click **Preview** in the **Array** dialog to view the changes in the viewport as you change settings in the dialog.

To understand the functioning of this tool, reset 3ds Max and create a teapot in the scene. Ensure teapot is selected in a viewport and then choose **Array** from the **Tools** menu to open the **Array** dialog. Now, click **Preview** and set other parameters as shown in Figure F5. Notice in Figure F5, 3ds Max creates **4** copies of the teapot with **60** units distance between each copy. Notice total distance is now **300** units, as shown in **Totals** section of the dialog indicating that **5** copies of the teapot are taking up **300** units space along the **X** direction.

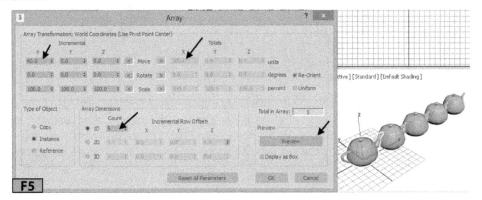

Now, if you want to distribute these teapots over a distance of say **400** units, click **>** on the right of the **Move** label and then set **X** to **400** [see Figure F6], the teapots are now spread over a distance of **400** units. Similarly, you can create an array using the **Rotate** and **Scale** transformations.

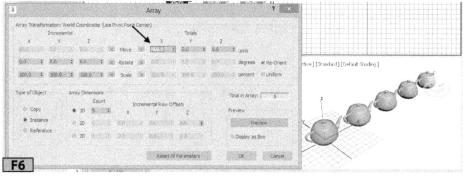

F6

Settings in Figures F7 and F8 show how you can create a 2D or 3D array, respectively, using the **Array** dialog.

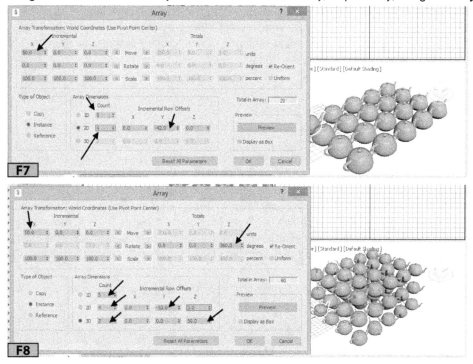

F7

F8

You can also create a **360** degree array using the **Array** dialog. Reset 3ds Max and then create a **Teapot** primitive with radius **10** at the top edge of the grid [see Figure F9]. From the **Main** toolbar | **User Center** flyout, choose **Use Transform Coordinate Center** [see Figure F10]. Choose **Array** from the **Tools** menu to open the **Array** dialog. Now, specify the settings, as shown in Figure F11 to create 12 teapots in a full circle [360 degrees].

Working with the Spacing Tool

This tool allows you to distribute the selected objects along a spline or along the distance specified by two points. You can also control the spacing between two objects. This tool can be activated by choosing **Tools | Align | Spacing Tool** from the menu bar or choosing **Spacing Tool** from the **Array** flyout.

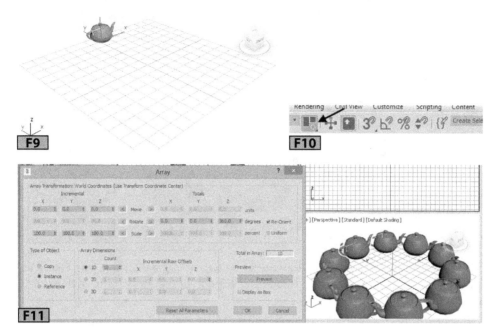

To distribute objects along a path, select the objects in the scene and then activate the **Spacing Tool** to open the **Spacing Tool** dialog [see Figure F12]. This dialog gives you two methods for selecting path: **Pick Path** and **Pick Points**. If you click **Pick Path**, place a cursor on a spline in the view and click to select the spline as path. Now, specify the number of objects you want to distribute and then choose a distribution algorithm from the drop-down available in the **Parameters** section [see Figure F13]. Turn on **Follow**, if you want to align the pivot points of the object along the tangents of the spline [see Figure F14].

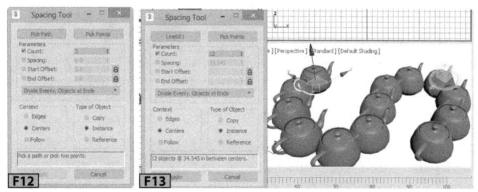

If you click **Pick Points** from the **Spacing Tool** dialog, specify the path by clicking on two places in the viewport. When you are finished with the tool, 3ds Max deletes the spline.

Working with Clone and Align Tool

This tool lets you distribute the source objects based on the current selection to a selection of the target objects. You can activate this tool by choosing **Align | Clone and Align** from the **Tools** menu. Alternatively, choose **Clone and Align Tool** from the **Array** flyout.

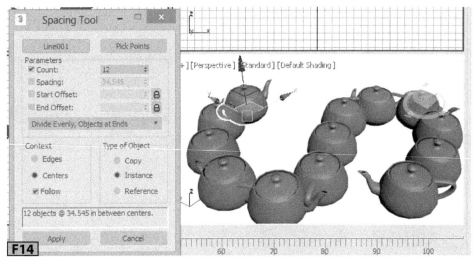

F14

To use the **Clone and Align** tool, create four teapots and a cone in the viewport [see Figure F15]. Select cone in a viewport and then choose **Align | Clone and Align** from the **Tools** menu to open the **Clone and Align** dialog.

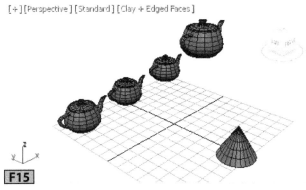

F15

In this dialog, click **Pick** and then click on each teapot to align the cone with the teapots [see Figure F16]. If you want to pick multiple destination objects at once, click **Pick List** to open the **Pick Destination Objects** dialog. In this dialog, select the objects and then click **Pick**.

Working With the Select and Place Tool

The **Select and Place** tool has been introduced in the 2015 release of 3ds Max. This tool is cousin of the **AutoGrid** option found in the **Object Type** rollout. However you can use it any time in your scene not just when you are creating an object. This tool can be activated by using one of the following four methods:

- Click the **Select and Place** icon on the **Main** toolbar.
- Choose **Placement** from the **Edit** menu.
- Press **Y** on the keyboard.
- RMB click on an object and then choose **Placement** from the **Transform** quadrant [see Figure F17].

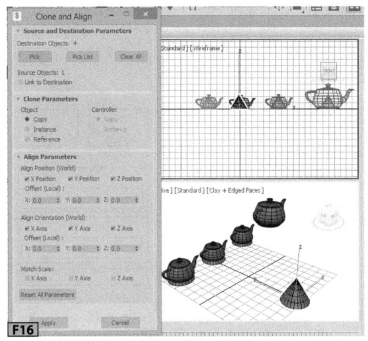

F16

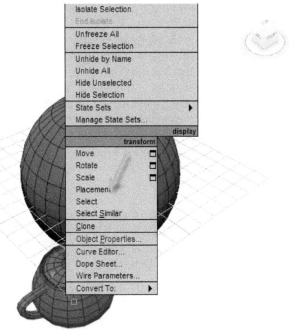

F17

To place an object, you don't have to select it first. Pick the **Select and Place** tool, click on the object to select it and then drag to place on another object [see Figure F18].

As you drag the object, the orientation of the object changes based on the normals of the target object and object **Up Axis** settings. The contact position of the target surface will be the object's pivot. To change the **Up Axis** settings, RMB click on the **Select and Place** tool on the **Main** toolbar to open the **Placement Settings** dialog [see Figure F19] and then select the axis from the **Object Up Axis** button array.

When **Rotate** is active on the **Placement Settings** dialog, the translation of the object is prevented and object rotates around the local axis speci- fied with the **Object Up Axis** settings. **Use Base as Pivot** is useful in those cases when the pivot is not already located in the base of the object. **Pillow Mode** is very useful when you are trying to place an object on a target whose surface is uneven. This option prevents the intersection of the objects. When **Autoparent** is active, the placed object automati- cally becomes the child of the other object. This is a quick way to make parent-child relationship.

Note: Select and Rotate tool
*If you just want to rotate the object, you can use the **Select and Rotate** tool from the **Main** toolbar.*

There are some more goodies associated with this tool:

- You can clone an object while dragging it by pressing **Shift**.
- Hold **Ctrl** and then drag to position an object vertically along the **Up Axis**.
- You can prevent an object from rotating while you place it by holding **Alt**.

You can also place several objects at one go. You can either select the desired objects before picking the **Select and Place** tool or you can select additional objects using **Ctrl** when this tool is active. Each object will move according to its own pivot, unless objects are linked together.

Working With the Select and Manipulate Tool

The **Select and Manipulate** tool allows you to interactively edit the parameters of certain objects by dragging the manipulators in the viewports. The state of this tool is non-exclusive. You can manipulate objects as long as any of the select mode or one of the transform mode is active but if you want to select a manipulator helper, you must deactivate the **Select and Manipulate** tool. All those primitives with a **Radius** parameter have a built-in manipulator for the radius value. Let's see how it works:

Create a **Teapot** primitive in the scene. Pick the **Select and Manipulate** tool from the **Main** toolbar. A green ring appears beneath the teapot [see Figure F20]. Click drag the ring to interactively change the radius of the teapot. Click on **Select and Manipulate** on the **Main** toolbar to deactivate the tool. There are three types of custom manipulators available in 3ds Max: cone angle manipulator, plane angle manipulator, and slider manipulator. The cone angle manipulator is used by a spot light's **Hotspot** and **Falloff** controls. To create a cone angle manipulator, choose **Create** panel | **Helpers** | **Manipulators** and then click **Cone Angle**. Click drag in the viewport to create the helper [see Figure F21]. To change its parameters, go to **Modify** panel and change the values.

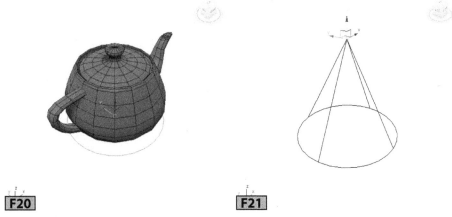

F20   F21

Now, let's work on a spot light to see this manipulator in action:

Create a **Teapot** primitive in the scene. Now create a spot light and place it as shown in Figure F22. Ensure the spot light is selected and then click **Select and Manipulate** from the **Main** toolbar. Two rings appear on the spot light [see Figure F23].

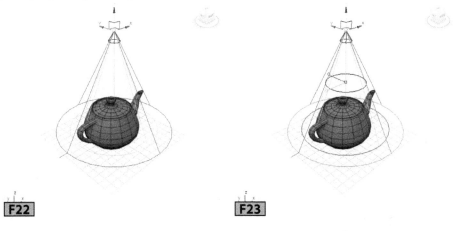

F22   F23

The inner ring controls **Hotspot** whereas the outer rings controls **Falloff**. Click drag to interactively change these parameters. The plane angle manipulator allows you to create a lever or joystick type shape. You can use its **Angle** parameter to create a custom control. You can use this control to drive parameter of another objects.

Let's see how it works, choose **Create** panel | **Helpers** | **Manipulators** and then click **Plane Angle**. In the **Front** viewport, click drag to create a shape [see Figure F24]. The **Plane Angle** manipulator always created vertically along the Y axis of the viewport in which you are creating it. Create a teapot in the **Perspective** viewport. Ensure the **Select and Manipulate** tool is not active and manipulator is selected. Choose **Wire Parameters** | **Wire Parameters** from the **Animation** menu. In the popup that appears, choose **Object (Plane Angle Manipulator)** | **Angle** [Figure F25]. A rubber band line appears. Click on the teapot.

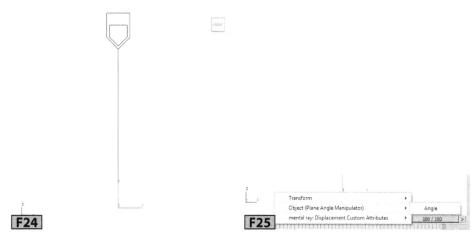

In the popup that appears, choose **Object (Teapot)** | **Radius** [see Figure F26]. In the **Parameter Wiring** dialog, click **One-way connection** button and then the **Connect** button [see Figure F27] to make the connection. Now close the dialog.

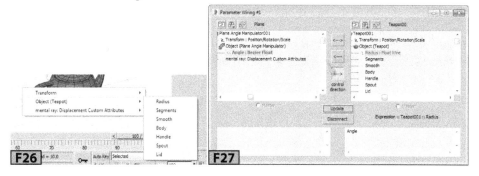

Pick the **Select and Manipulate** tool and click drag the manipulator to interactively change the radius of the teapot. The third type of manipulator, **Slider**, which creates a graphic control in the viewport. You can wire its value to a parameter of another object within the scene.

Here's how:

Create a **Slider** manipulator in the **Front** viewport. Create a teapot in the **Perspective** viewport [see Figure F28].Wire the **Value** parameter to the **Radius** of the teapot as described above. Change the controls such as **Label**, **Minimum**, and **Maximum** values in the **Modify** panel [see Figure F29]. Pick the **Select and Manipulate** tool and drag the manipulator's **Adjust** control to interactively change the shape of the teapot. Figure F30 shows the components of a **Slider** control [1. Label, 2. Value, 3. Move, 4. Show/hide, 5. Slider bar, 6. Adjust value, and 7. Change width].

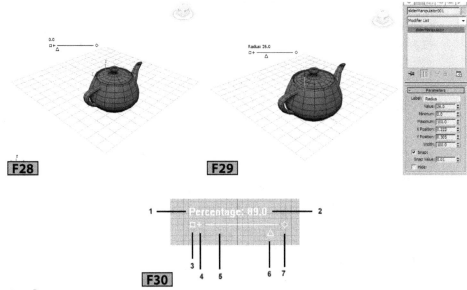

Scene Explorer

The **Scene Explorer** [see Figure F31] is a modeless dialog in 3ds Max that you can use to view, sort, filter, and select objects. In addition, you can rename, delete, hide, and freeze objects. You can also create and modify and edit object properties en masse. Each workspace in 3ds Max comes with a different **Scene Explorer** with the same name as its workspace. The **Scene Explorer** is docked to the left of the viewports.

Several explorers in 3ds Max are different versions of the **Scene Explorer**. These includes: **Layer Explorer**, **Container Explorer**, **MassFX Explorer**, and **Material Explorer**. The **Scene Explorer** comes with many toolbars [see Figure F31]. Table 2 summarizes various toolbars available.

Table 2: The **Scene Explorer** toolbars	
Flag	**Toolbar**
1	Selection toolbar
4	View toolbar
5	Display toolbar
6	Find toolbar
7	Tools toolbar

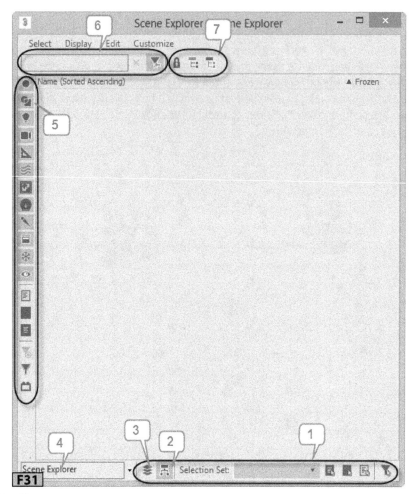

Selection Toolbar

The **Scene Explorer** comes with two sorting modes: **Sort By Layer** mode and **Sort By Hierarchy** mode. You can use the **Sort By Layer** or **Sort by Hierarchy** button on the **Selection** toolbar [marked as 1 in Figure F31] to use these modes. The **Sort By Layer** button [marked as 2 in Figure F31] sets **Scene Explorer** to **Sort By Layer** mode. In this mode, you can use drag and drop feature for editing layers. Some other options are also available in this mode. The **Sort By Hierarchy** [marked as 3 in Figure F31] button allows you to edit hierarchies using drag and drop functionality.

If you click on an object in the **Scene Explorer**, the object is selected and the associated row in the explorer gets highlighted. To select multiple objects, click on objects with the **Ctrl** held down. Press **Ctrl+A** to select all objects, **Ctrl+I** to invert the selection, and **Ctrl+D** to deselect. These commands are also available at the right of the **Selection** toolbar [marked as 1 in Figure 31]. The **Selection Set** drop-down in the **Selection** toolbar lets you select objects using **Named Selection Sets**.

Tools Toolbar

The tools available in this toolbar are dependent on whether **Sort By Hierarchy** mode or **Sort By Layer** mode is active. When **Lock Cell Editing** is on, you cannot change any name or settings. The **Pick Parent** button is only available in the **Sort By Hierarchy** mode. It allows you to change the parent. To make an object parent, select one or more objects and then click **Pick Parent**. Now, select the object that you want parent of the selected object. The **Create New Layer** button is available in the **Sort By Layer** mode. When you click **Create New Layer**, a new layer is created and the selection is automatically added to this layer. The new layer you create becomes the active layer and any subsequent objects you create are added to this layer automatically. If an existing layer is selected, and you click **Create New Layer**, the new layer becomes child of the selected layer. The **Add to Active Layer** is available in the **Sort By Layer** mode only. When you click on this button, all selected objects and layers are assigned to the active layer. **Select Children** allows you to select all child objects and layers of the selected items.

Tip: Selecting children
Double-clicking on a parent layer or object selects the parent and all its children.

The **Make Selected Layer Active** button is available in the **Sort By Layer** mode only. When you click on this button, 3ds Max makes the selected layer the active layer. Alternatively, click on the layer icon to make it the layer active.

Display Toolbar

The **Display** toolbar allows you to display various categories in the **Scene Explorer**. It controls the type of objects that appear in the **Scene Explorer's** listing. You can also solo the category by clicking on one of the category button with **Alt** held down. You can also turn on or off the categories by choosing **Display | Object Types** from the **Scene Explorer's** menu bar.

View Toolbar

The **View** toolbar is located at the bottom-left corner of the **Scene Explorer**. This toolbar shows the name of the current **Scene Explorer**. When you click on the arrow located in this toolbar, a menu appears. This menu gives access to all local and global explorers.

Local and Global Scene Explorers

3ds Max comes with different **Scene Explorer** configurations. These configurations are available to every scene you create in 3ds Max. Therefore, they are referred to as **Global Scene Explorers**. On the other hand the **Local Scene Explorers** live within a single scene and saved/loaded with the scene. The options to make a **Local** explorer **Global** are available in the menu located on the **View** toolbar [see Figure F32].

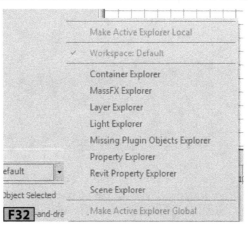

Q. How to delete objects?

To delete one or more objects in the **Scene Explorer**, select them and then press **Delete** or RMB click on the list and then choose **Delete** from the **Quad** menu.

Q. How to hide and show objects?

Click the light bulb icon of the layer or object to hide. The light bulb icon turns gray. Click again to reveal.

Q. How to create hierarchies in the Sort By Hierarchy mode?

To make a parent, drag and drop the child objects' name or icon onto the object that you want to act as parent. To restore the child object to the top level, drag them to an empty area of the **Scene Explorer**. Alternatively, you can RMB click on them and then choose **Unlink** from the **Quad** menu. You can use the same techniques on the layers as well.

Q. How to freeze objects?

To freeze objects, click on the **Frozen** column of the object. Click again to unfreeze. If you want to freeze many objects, select them and then click on the **Frozen** column of any selected objects.

Q. How to change object properties?

To change the object properties, select one or more objects in the **Scene Explorer** and then RMB. Choose **Properties** from the **Quad** menu to open the **Object Properties** dialog. You can use this dialog to change the properties of the selected objects.

Q. How to rename an object?

Select the object and then RMB click. Choose **Rename** from the **Quad** menu and then type a new name for the object.

Tip: Renaming objects

*Slowly double-click on the object name to rename the object if you don't want to use the **Quad** menu.*

Q. Can I add more column next to the Frozen column?

Yes, you can. RMB click on any of the column head and then choose **Configure Columns** [see Figure F33] from the popup menu. The **Configure Column** window appears [see Figure F34]. Click on the name of the column in this window that you want to add. Figure F35 shows the **Has Material** column. A tick will appear in this column if the material has been assigned to the object.

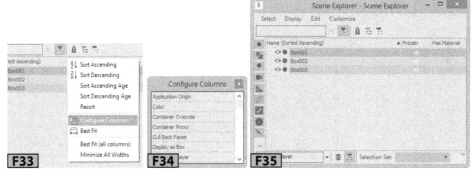

Q. Can I search object by names?

Yes, you can search object by using the search text box available in the **Find** toolbar. Type the search sting and press **Enter**. For example, if you have many teapots in the scene and all have default names. Entering **tea** in the **search** field and then pressing **Enter** will select all teapots in the scene. You can also use the wild card characters **?** and ***** to create a broader search criteria.

Working with the Precision Tools

3ds Max comes with several tools and objects that allow you to position and align objects efficiently. Two tools [**Select and Place** tool, and **Select and Manipulate** tool] I have already discussed that let you align and position objects. You have also seen the use of some helpers that are used with the **Select and Manipulate** tool.

Using Units

The units define the measurement system for the scene. The default unit system in 3ds Max is **Generic**. Besides the **Generic** units, you can also use feet and inches units both decimal and fractional. The **Metric** system allows you to specify units from millimeters to kilometers. You can specify the unit system from the **Units Setup** dialog [see Figure F36]. You can open this dialog by choosing **Units Setup** from the **Customize** menu. On clicking **System Unit Setup** from this dialog, the **System Unit Setup** dialog appears from where you can specify the **System** units.

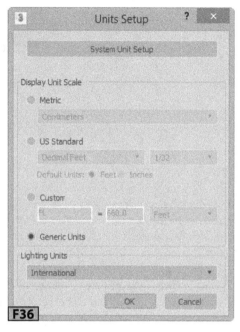

F36

Q. What is the difference between Scene Units and System Units?

The system units only affects how geometry appears in the viewports whereas the system units control the actual scale of the geometry.

Caution: System Units
*The system units should only be changed before you create your scene or import a **unitless** file. Do not change the system units in the current scene.*

If you change units for a scene, 3ds Max automatically changes the values for the controls. For example, if you are using **Centimeters**, and value in a spinner is **30** cm, when you change units to **Decimal Inches**; 3ds Max will change the value to **11.811** inches. Now, if you type **50cm** in the spinner and press **Enter**, 3ds Max will change value to **19.685** inches. Similarly, if you type **2'** in the spinner, the value will be changed to **24.0** inches.

Using Grids

Grids are two dimensional arrays that you can use to position the objects accurately. You can use grids to visualize space, scale, and distance. You can use it as construction plane to create objects as well use it for snapping objects using the snap feature. I will discuss snap features later in this unit. 3ds Max provides two types of grids: **Home** grid and **Grid** objects.

Home Grid

The **Home** grid is defined by three intersecting planes along the world **X**, **Y**, and **Z** axes. These planes intersect at the origin defined by **0,0,0**. The **Home** grid is fixed, you cannot move or rotate it.

Tip: Home Grid
*Press **G** to toggle the visibility of the **Home** grid.*

Grid Object

The **Grid** object [see Figure F37] is a helper object that you can use to create a reference grid as per your needs. You can create as many **Grid** objects as you want in a scene. However, only one **Grid** object will be active at a time. When a **Grid** object is active, it replaces the **Home** grid in all viewports. You can rename and delete **Grid** objects like any other object. The **Grid** object is available in the **Helpers** category on the **Create** panel.

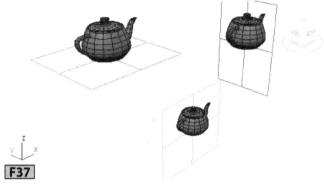

F37

Tip: Activating the Home grid and Grid object
*You can activate the **Home** grid by choosing **Grids and Snaps** | **Activate Home Grid** from the **Tools** menu. When you choose this command, it activates the **Home** grid in all viewports and deactivates the current active grid object. Similarly, you can activate a **Grid** object by choosing **Grids and Snaps** | **Activate Grid Object** from the **Tools** menu.*

Tip: Aligning a Grid object to the view
*To align a **Grid** object with the current view, choose **Grids and Snaps** | **Activate Grid Object** from the **Quad** menu. The **Grid** object is aligned and will be coplanar with the current view.*

Auto Grid

The **Auto Grid** feature lets you create objects on the surface of other objects. The **Auto Grid** option is available on the **Object Type** rollout of any category. It is also available in the **Extras** toolbar. When you activate this option, and drag the cursor on the surface of an object, a construction plane is created temporarily on the surface of object.

Tip: Select and Place tool
*The **Select and Place** tool discussed earlier provides a similar mechanism to align the objects.*

Aligning Objects

3ds Max provides six different tools for aligning the objects in a scene. These tools are available in the **Align** flyout on the **Main** toolbar.

Using with Align Tool

The **Align** tool in 3ds Max allows you to align the current selection to a target selection. You can pick the **Align** tool from the **Align** flyout on the **Main** toolbar. You can also activate this tool by choosing **Align** | **Align** from the **Tools** menu or by pressing **Alt+A**. Using this tool, you can align the position and orientation of the bounding box of a source object to the bounding box of a target object. A bounding box is the smallest box that encloses the extents (maximum dimensions) of an object. A bounding box appears when you set a viewport to non-wireframe mode. Figure F38 shows the extents of a teapot model.

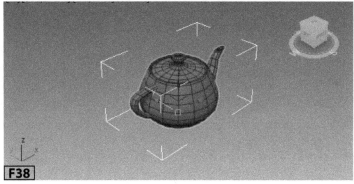

F38

To show the bounding box, select the object and then press **J**. You can also enable display of the bounding boxes by turning on **Selection Brackets** from the **Viewport Setting and Preference** dialog | **Per-View Preferences** panel [see Figure F39]. Refer to Explore More section of **Unit MI1** for more information on **Viewport Setting and Preference** dialog.

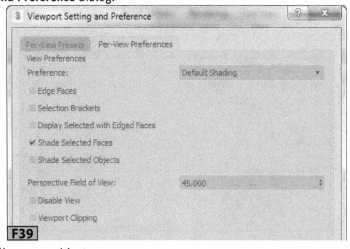

F39

Let's dive in and align some objects:

Create three boxes and assign them red, green, and blue colors [see Figure F40]. Use the following dimensions:

Red Box: Length=52, Width=61, and Height=32
Green Box: Length=35, Width=40, and Height=12
Blue Box: Length=50, Width=40, and Height=30

RMB click on the red box and choose **Object Properties** from the **Quad** menu. On the **General panel** | **Display Properties** group, turn on **See-Through**. This will help you better see the alignment process. Now let's center align the red and blue boxes along the **X** and **Y** axes. Make sure the red box is selected and then pick the **Align** tool from the **Main** toolbar. Click the blue box. On the **Align Selection dialog** | **Align Position (World) group**, turn on **X Position** and **Y Position**. Turn off **Z Position**. Make sure **Center** is on in the **Current Object** and **Target Object** groups. You will see that both the objects are center aligned [see Figure F41]. Click **OK** to accept changes.

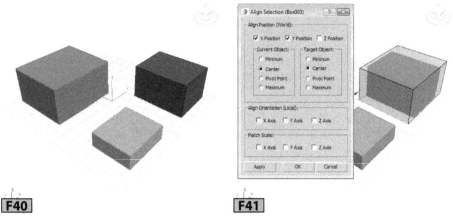

F40 F41

Now, let's see how to place blue box on the top of the red box.

Select the blue box and then pick the **Align** tool from the **Main** toolbar. Click red box. We have already performed alignment along the **X** and **Y** axes. Therefore, turn off **X Position** and **Y Position** and turn on **Z Position**. You will see that now the blue box is at the center of the red box. Turn on **Maximum** from the **Target Object** group. Notice the blue box's center is aligned to the center of the red box [see Figure 42]. Now select **Pivot Point** from the **Current Object** group. The blue box sits on the top of the red box [see Figure F43]. Click **OK** to accept changes.

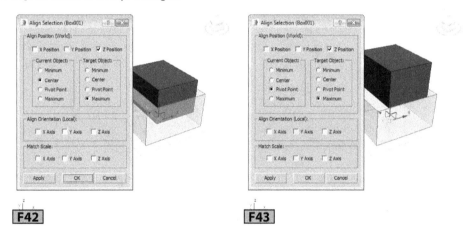

F42　　　　　　　　F43

Now, let's align one corner of the green box with blue box.

Select the green box and then pick the **Align** tool from the **Main** toolbar. Click the blue box. Turn on **X Position**, **Y Position**, and **Z Position**. Turn on **Minimum** from the **Current Object** and **Target Object** groups [see Figure F44]. Click **OK** to accept changes. With the green box selected, click the blue box using the **Align** tool. Now, turn on **Z Position** and turn off **X Position** and **Y Position**. Turn on **Maximum** from the **Target Object** group and click **OK**. The boxes are now stacked over each other [see Figure F45].

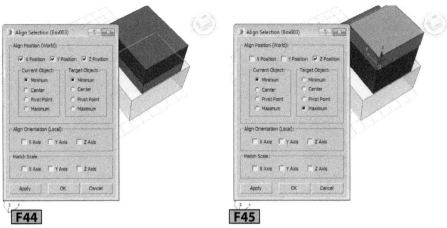

F44   F45

Using the Quick Align Tool

The **Quick Align** tool instantly aligns an object with the target object. The hotkeys associated with this tool are **Shift+A**. To align an object, select the source object and press **Shift+A** to activate the tool. Now, click on the target object to align two objects [see Figure F46]. If the current selection contains a single object, this tool uses the pivot points of the two objects for alignment. If multiple objects are selected, the selection center of the source objects is aligned with the pivot of the target objects.

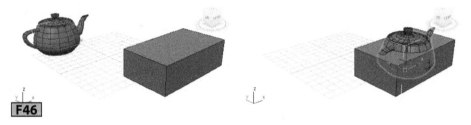

F46

Using the Normal Align Tool

This tool allows you to align the two objects based on the directions of the normals of the selected faces. The hotkeys associated with this tool are **Alt+N**. To understand functioning of this tool, create a sphere and teapot in the scene [see Figure F47]. Select the teapot, the source object in this case. Press **Alt+N** to activate the tool and then drag across the surface of the teapot, a blue arrow indicates the location of the current normal [see Figure F48]. Keep dragging on the surface until you find the normal you are looking for. Now, click and drag on the surface of the sphere until you find the normal to which you want to align the the source object. Release the mouse button the teapot gets aligned with the sphere [see Figure 49] and the **Normal Align** dialog opens. Using the controls available in this dialog you can offset the position and orientation of the teapot.

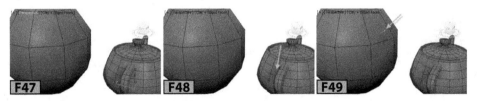

F47   F48   F49

Q. What are normals?

*A normal is a vector that defines the inner and outer surfaces of a face in a mesh. The direction of the vector indicates the front [outer] surface of a face or vertex. Sometimes, normals are flipped during the modeling process. To fix this issue, you can use the **Normal** modifier to flip or unify normals. Figure 50 shows the vertex and face normals, respectively.*

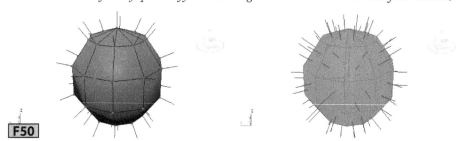

F50

Using the Place Highlight Tool

You can use this tool to align an object or light to another object so that its highlight [reflection] can be precisely positioned. To position a light to highlight a face, make sure the viewport that you want to render is active. Choose **Place Highlight** from the **Align** flyout and drag the mouse pointer on the object to place the highlight. Now, release the mouse button when the normal indicates the face on which you want to place the highlight [see Figure F51].

Note: Light type and highlights

With the omni, free spot, or directional light, 3ds Max displays face normal. With a target spotlight, 3ds Max displays target of the light and base of it's cone.

Using the Align Camera Tool

This tool lets you align the camera to a selected face normal. This tool works similar to the **Place Highlight** tool but it does not change the camera position interactively. You need to release the mouse button and then 3ds Max aligns the camera with the selected face.

Using the Align View Tool

When this tool is picked from the **Align** flyout, it opens the **Align to View** dialog that lets you align the local axis of the selection or sub-object selection with the current viewport [see Figure F52]. To use this tool, select the objects or sub-objects to align and then choose **Align to View** from the **Align** flyout. 3ds Max opens the **Align to View** dialog. Choose the options from the dialog as desired. If you want to flip the direction of alignment, turn on **Flip** on this dialog box.

Drawing Assistants

3ds Max provides several tools and utilities that help you in drawing objects with precession. Let's have a look.

F51   F52

Measuring Distances

The **Measure Distance** tool allows you to quickly calculate distance between two points. The calculated distance appears in the **Status Bar** in Scene [display] units. To measure distance, choose **Measure Distance** from the **Tools** menu. Now, click on the point in the viewport from where you want to measure the distance. Click again in the viewport where you want to measure to. The distance between the two points is displayed in the **Status Bar**.

The **Measure** utility available in the **Utilities** panel provides the measurement of a selected object or spline. To measure an object, select the object and then on the **Utilities** panel | **Measure** rollout, click **Measure**. The measurements are displayed in the **Measure** rollout [see Figure F53].

There is one more utility called **Rescale World Units** that you can use to rescale the word units. You can scale entire scene or the selected objects. To rescale an object, select it and then on the **Utilities** panel click **More** to open the **Utilities** panel. Select **Rescale World Units** from the dialog and then click **OK**. The **Rescale World Units** rollout appears in the **Utilities** panel. Click **Rescale** from this rollout to open the **Rescale World Units** dialog [see Figure F54].

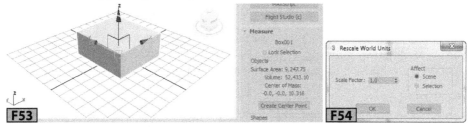

Set **Scale Factor** in this dialog and then turn on **Scene** or **Selection** from the **Affect** section. Click **OK** to apply the scale factor to the selected object or to entire scene. For example, you specify **Scale Factor** as **2** and turn on **Selection** from the dialog, the selected object will be scaled to double of its current size.

Using Snaps

The Snap tools in 3ds Max allow you to precisely control the dimensions and placement of the objects when you create or transform them. You and invoke these tools using the **Snap** buttons available on the **Main** toolbar. You can also invoke these tools by choosing **Grids and Snaps** from the **Tools** menu.

2D Snap, 2.5 Snap, and 3D Snap

The hotkey for activating snap is **S**. The **2D Snap** tool snaps the cursor to the active construction grid including the geometry on the plane of the grid. The **Z** axis is ignored by this tool. The **2.5D Snap** tool snaps the cursor to the vertices or edges of the projection of an object onto the active grid. The **3D snap** is the default tool. It snaps the cursor directly to any geometry in the 3D space.

RMB click on snap toggle button to open the **Grid and Snap Settings** dialog [see Figure F55]. You can specify which type of snap of you want active from the **Snap** panel of this dialog box.

Fox example, if you want the cursor to snap to the pivot or vertices of the object, turn on **Pivot** and **Vertex** from this panel.

To see snap in action, turn on **Pivot** and **Vertex** from the **Grid and Snap Settings** dialog. Now, create a box and teapot in the viewport [see first image at the left of Figure F56].

Pick the **Move** tool from the **Main** toolbar and move the teapot to one of the vertex of the box or its pivot [see middle and right image in Figure F57].

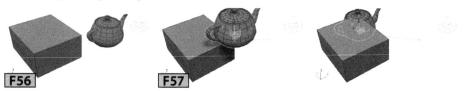

Angle Snap Toggle

You can use the **Angle Snap Toggle** to rotate an object around a given axis in the increment you set. This snap toggle also works with the **Pan/Orbit** camera controls, **FOV** and **Roll** camera settings, and **Hotspot/Falloff** spotlight angles. The hotkey for invoking this toggle is **A**.

To rotate an object, click **Angle Snap Toggle** on the **Main** toolbar and then rotate the object using the **Rotate** tool. By default, the rotation takes place in five degree increments. You can change this default value by specifying a value for the **Angle** control in the **Options** panel of the **Grid and Snap Settings** dialog.

Percent Snap Toggle

The **Percent Snap Toggle** lets you control the increments of scaling by the specified percentage. The hotkey for invoking this toggle is **Shift+Ctrl+P**. The default percentage value is **10**. You can change this default value by specifying a value for the **Percent** control in the **Options** panel of the **Grid and Snap Settings** dialog.

Spinner Snap Toggle

This toggle allows you to set single-increment or decrement value for all the spinners in 3ds Max. The default value is **1**. To change this value, RMB click on **Spinner Snap Toggle** on the **Main** toolbar to open the **Preferences Settings** dialog. In the **Spinners** section of the **General** panel, specify a value for the **Snap** control.

Modifiers

The modifiers in 3ds Max provide a way to edit and sculpt objects. You can change shape of an object using the modifier's properties. Figure F58 shows the original box [first image] and the modified geometry after applying the **Bend**, **Twist**, and **Taper** modifiers, respectively.

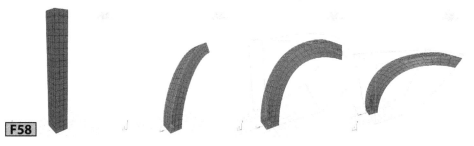

You can apply modifiers from the **Modifier** drop-down available in the **Modify** panel of **Command Panel** [see Figure F59]. The modifier you apply to an object are stored in a stack called modifier stack.

Practical Test

Complete the following test:

Test 1: Creating a Robo Model

Create a robot model, as shown in Figure P1, using the **Standard** primitives.

Hints:

- The primitives used in the model shown in Figure P1 are: **Box**, **Sphere**, **Cylinder**, **Pyramid**, **Cone**, **Torus**, and **Pipe**.
- The fingers are created using **Torus** primitives. Turn on **Slice On** the **Parameters** rollout of torus to create opening in the torus.
- Use **Auto Grid** and **Select and Place** features of 3ds Max to align and place body parts.
- Create one leg and then use the **Mirror** tool to create a copy on the other side. Apply same concept on eyes and hands. Create a group before applying the **Mirror** tool.
- Create layers for different parts in the **Layer Explorer**. For example, keep all geometries that make hand in the hands layer, and so forth.
- Try to use various features of the **Scene Explorer**.

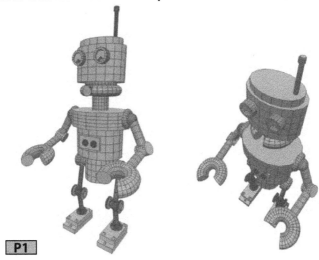

P1

Summary

The unit covered the following topics:

- Working with templates
- Creating clones and duplicates
- Understanding hierarchies

- Working with the **Scene** and **Layer** Explorers
- Understanding the **Mirror**, **Select and Place**, and **Select and Manipulate** tools
- Working with the **Align** and **Array** tools
- Working with precision and drawing aids
- Understanding modifiers, and normals

Unit MT1-Material Editors

A material editor is a dialog that allows you to create, and edit materials as well as to assign them to the objects in the scene. A material in 3ds Max defines how light is reflected and transmitted by the objects in a scene.

In the unit, I will describe the following:

- **Compact Material Editor**
- **Slate Material Editor**

3ds Max offers two material editors, **Compact Material Editor** and **Slate Material Editor**. These editors offer a variety of the functions and features that allow you to design realistic looking surfaces in 3ds Max. To open an editor, choose **Compact** or **Slate** option from the **Material Editor** flyout on the **Main** toolbar. You can also open an editor by choosing **Compact Material Editor** or **Slate Material Editor** from the **Rendering** menu | **Material Editor** sub-menu | **Compact Material Editor/Slate Material Editor**. If you are using the enhanced menu system, these options are in the **Material** menu | **Create/Edit Materials** sub-menu.

Compact Material Editor

This was the only material editor available prior to the 2011 release of 3ds Max. It is comparatively a small dialog [see Figure F1] than the **Slate Material Editor** and allows you to quickly preview the material. If you are assigning materials that have already been designed, this material editor is the preferred choice.

Note: Additional Features
*The **Compact Material Editor** has some options such as **Video Color Check** and **Custom Sample Objects** that are not available in the **Slate Material Editor**.*

The **Compact Material Editor's** interface consists of menu bar at the top [see Figure F1], sample slots below the menu bar, and toolbars at the bottom and right of the sample slots. Now onward, I will refer to these toolbars as horizontal and vertical toolbars, respectively. The interface also contains many rollouts. The content on these rollouts depends on the active material slot and the type of material it hosts.

Note: Switching Editors
*If you want to switch to **Slate Material Editor**, choose **Slate Material Editor** from the editor's **Modes** menu.*

Sample Slots

The sample slots allow you to preview material and maps. By default, six sample slots appear in the editor. You can increase the number of slots by choosing **Cycle 3x2, 5x3, 6x4 Sample Slots** from the editor's **Options** menu. This option cycles through the 3x2, 5x3, and 6x4 slots arrangement. To make a sample slot active, click on the sample slot. The active sample slot appears with a white border around it.

*The **Compact Material Editor** allows you to edit up to 24 material at a time. However, the scene might contain an unlimited numbers of materials. When you finish a material and apply it to the objects in the scene. You can use the slot occupied by that material to design the next material.*

By default, material appears on a sphere geometry in a sample slot. You can change the sphere to cylinder or cube by choosing the desired option from the **Sample Type** flyout. This flyout is the first entry in the editor's vertical toolbar. To view a magnified version of the sample slot in a floating window, double-click on it. You can resize the window to change the magnification level of the sample slot.

Hot and Cool Materials

A sample slot is considered to be hot if it is assigned to one or more surfaces in the scene. When you use the editor to adjust properties of a hot material the changes are reflected in the viewport at the same time. The corners of a sample slot indicates whether the material is hot or not. Here are the possibilities:

No triangle: The material is not used in the scene.
Outlined white triangle: The material is hot and the changes you make to it will change the material displayed in the scene.
Solid white triangle: The material is not only hot but it is also applied to the currently selected object in the scene.

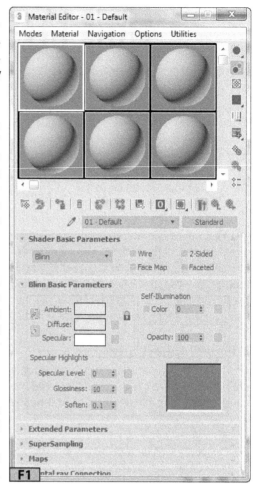

Notice the three sample slots in Figure F2 that shows three possibilities: a hot material applied to the currently selected, a hot material is applied to the scene but not on the currently selected object, and a cool material which is active but not assigned to scene, respectively. If you want to make a hot material cool, click **Make Material Copy** from the horizontal toolbar. You can have the same material with the same name in multiple slots but only one slot can be hot. However, you can have more than one hot sample slot as long as each sample slot has a different material.

Note: Dragging a material

If you drag a material to copy it from one sample slot to another, the destination slot will be cool whereas the original slot remains hot.

When you RMB click on a sample slot, a popup menu appears. Table 1 summarizes the options available in this menu.

Table 1: Sample slot RMB click menu	
Option	Description
Drag/Copy	This is on by default. When on, dragging a sample slot copies the material from one sample slot to another.
Drag/Rotate	When you select this option, dragging the sample slot rotates the sample geometry in the slot. This is useful in visualizing the map in the slot.
Reset Rotation	Resets the sample slot's rotation.
Render Map	Opens the **Render Map** dialog that allows you to render the current map. You can create an **AVI** file if the map is animated.
Options	Opens the material editor's options.
Magnify	Generates a magnified view of the current sample slot.
Select By Material	Selects objects based on the material in the sample slot.
Highlight Assets in the ATS dialog	This option is typically used for the bitmap textures. It opens the **Asset Tracking** dialog with the assets highlighted.
Sample Windows Options	You can use these options to change the number of slots displayed in the material editor.

Managing Materials with the Compact Material Editor

By default, the **Standard** material is displayed when you select a sample slot. If you want to use the **Standard** material, you can choose the desired shading model from the drop-down available in the **Shader Basic Parameters** rollout of the editor and then assign colors or maps to the various components of the material. For example, if you want to assign a map to the **Diffuse** component of the material, click on the button located at the right of the **Diffuse** color swatch to open the **Material/Map Browser** which is a modeless dialog. From the browser, select the map from the **Maps | General/Scanline/Environment** rollout and then click **OK**.

Tip: Material Map Browser
You can also double-click on a map to select it and close the browser.

For example, if you want to apply a checker map, double-click on the **Checker** map from the **Maps | General** rollout of the browser. Once you select the map, 3ds Max shows rollouts in the editor that you can use to edit the properties of the map. To go back to the parent level, click **Go To Parent** from the horizontal toolbar.

You can also copy map from one component to another component. For example, you have applied a map to the **Diffuse** component of the material and you want to copy it to **Opacity** component. Drag the **Diffuse's** button onto the **Opacity's** button, the **Copy (Instance) Map** dialog appears. Select the desired option from the **Method** group and then click **OK** to create an instance, a copy, or just to swap the materials from one slot to another.

Note: Other materials
*If you want to use any other material than the **Standard** material, click on **Type** button [currently labelled as **Standard**] to open the **Material/Map Browser**. Double-click on the desired material from the **Materials | General/Scanline** rollout; the **Replace Material** dialog appears with options to discard the old material or keep the old material as a sub-material. Choose the desired option and click **OK**. The label **Standard** on the button will be replaced by the type of the new material. For example, if you have chosen **Blend**, the **Standard** label will be replaced by the **Blend** label.*

By default, 3ds Max gives a name to each material. This appears name below the horizontal toolbar. If you want to change the name, edit the name in the field. The name field only displays 16 characters but the material name can be longer than 16 characters.

If the material you want to change is present in the scene but is not displayed in any of the sample slots, you can get it directly from the scene. To do this, select the object in the scene and click a sample slot to make it active. From the horizontal toolbar, click **Get Material** 🔳 to open the **Material/Map Browser**. Find the scene material in the **Scene Materials** rollout and then double-click on the name of the material. You can also drag the material name to the sample slot. When you get a material from the scene, it is initially a hot material.

To apply a material to the objects in the scene, drag the sample slot that contains the material to the object[s] in the scene. If there is only one object selected in the scene, the material is immediately applied to that object. If there are more than one objects in the scene, 3ds Max prompts you to choose whether to apply the material to the single object or to the whole selection. You can also apply material to the selection by clicking **Assign Material To Selection** 🔳 on the horizontal toolbar. Once you apply material to objects in the scene, click **Show Shaded Material in Viewport** 🔳 on the horizontal toolbar to view the material on the objects in the scene.

Tip: Hot material
When you apply a material to an object, the material becomes a hot material.

Tip: Removing material from an object
*To remove a material from an object, select the object and then execute the following command from the **MAXScript Listener**: $.material=undefined.*

Note: Selecting objects that have the same material applied
*From the vertical toolbar, click **Select By Material** 🔳. This button will not be available unless the active sample slot contains a material that is applied to the objects in the scene. The **Select Objects** dialog appears. Those objects onto which the material has been applied appear highlighted in the dialog. Click **Select** to select the objects in the scene.*

You can also save a material to the library. A material library helps you in organizing materials. You can use a material from a library in another scene, if required. To save a material to the library, on the horizontal toolbar, click **Put To Library** 🔳, the **Put To Library** dialog appears. In this dialog, change the name of the material or leave as is. Click **OK** to save the material. The material is saved in the currently opened library. If no library is open, a new library is created. You can save this library as a file using the **Material/Map Browser** controls.

To get a material from the library, click **Get Material** 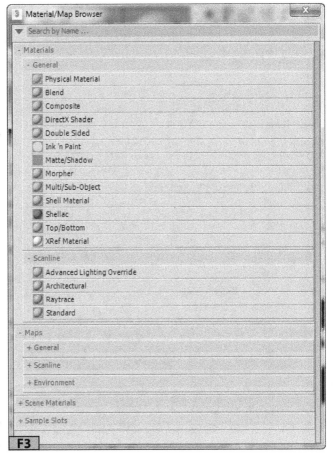 to open the **Material/Map Browser**. Now, open a library group. In the list of the materials in the library, double-click on the name of the material that you intend to use. The material you choose from the library replaces the material in the active sample slot.

Material/Map Browser

The **Material/Map Browser** [see Figure F3] allows you to choose a material, map, or mental ray shader. When you click the **Type** button or any button on the **Compact Material Editor**, a modal version of the **Material/Map Browser** opens.

Note: Slate Material Editor
*In the **Slate Material Editor**, the **Material/Map Browser** appears as a panel and always visible.*

At the top-left corner of the browser, the **Material/Map Browser Options** button is available. When you click this button, a menu is displayed from where you can set various options for the **Material/Map Browser**. The **Search by Name** field on the right of the button allows you to filter the maps and materials in the browser. For example, if you type **grad** in the field and press **Enter**, the maps and materials will be displayed below the field whose names start with the characters **grad** [see Figure F4].

The main part of the browser is the list of materials and maps arranged in the rollouts [groups]. You can collapse or expand these groups.

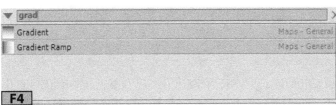

Note: Creating custom groups

*You can also create custom groups in the browser. To create a group, open the **Material/Map Browser Options*** *▼ menu and then choose **New Group**. The **Create New Group** dialog appears. In this dialog, type the name of the group and click **OK**. Now, you can drag the materials or maps from other groups and drop on the new group.*

Caution: Materials and maps in the Material/Map Browser

*By default, the **Material/Map Browser** only displays those maps and materials that are compatible with the active renderer.*

Note: Material/Map Browser's contextual menu

When you RMB click on the header of a rollout, a popup menu appears [see Figure F5]. This menu shows the general options related to that particular group.

Material Explorer

The **Material Explorer** [see Figure F6] allows you to browse and manage all materials in a scene. You can open the explorer from the **Rendering** menu. If you are using the enhanced menu system, you can open it from the **Materials** menu | **Tools (Material Set)** sub-menu. You can also open it as an extended viewport. To do this, choose **Material Explorer** from the **Point-Of-View (POV) Viewport** label menu | **Extended Viewports**.

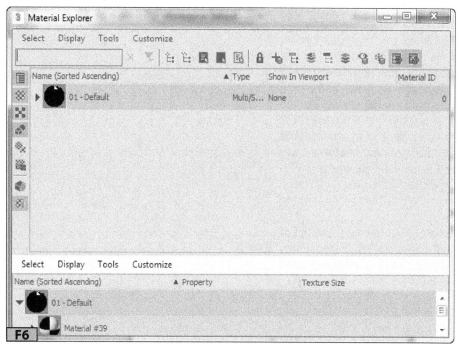

The **Compact Material Editor** lets you set the properties of the materials but there is limitations on number of materials it can display at a time. However, with the **Material Explorer**, you can browse all the materials in the scene. You can also see the objects onto which the materials are applied, you can change the material assignment, and manage materials in other ways.

Slate Material Editor

The **Slate Material Editor** is little complex than the **Compact Material Editor**. In this editor, the entities are displayed in form of nodes that you can wire together to create material trees. If you are working on a large scene with lots of materials, this editor is the preferred choice. The powerful search function provided by this editor, lets you find materials in a complex scene easily.

I mostly used the **Slate Material Editor** as its interface [see Figure F7] is more intuitive when it comes to designing materials. I have marked various components of the interface with numbers in Figure F7. Table 2 summarizes the **Slate Material Editor's** interface.

Number	Description
Table 2: The **Slate Material Editor's** interface overview	
Number	**Description**
1	Menu bar
2	Toolbar
3	Material/Map Browser
4	Status
5	Active View
6	View navigation
7	Parameter Editor
8	Navigator

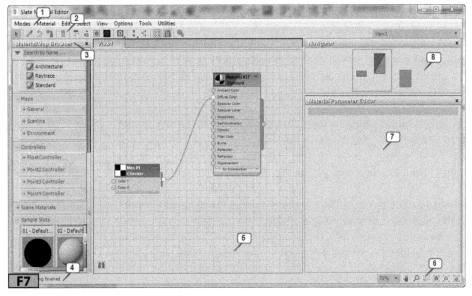

F7

There are three main visual elements of the **Slate Material Editor**: **Material/Map Browser**, **Active View**, and **Parameter Editor**. The **Active View** is the area where you create material trees and make connections between nodes using wires. The **Parameter Editor** is the area where you adjust settings of maps and materials.

You can float the components of the editor such as **Material/Map Browser**, or **Parameter Editor** [except view]. For example, to float the **Material/Map Browser**, double-click on its title. To dock it back to the editor, again double-click on its title.

Note: Preview window

By default, each material preview window opens as a floating window. When you dock a material preview window, it docks to the upper left area of the editor.

When you add materials or maps in the **Slate Material Editor**, they appear as nodes [see left image in Figure F8] in the active view.

You can then connect these nodes using wires to make material trees. A node has several components, here's is a quick rundown.

- The title bar of the node shows name of the material or map, material or map type, and a small preview icon of the material or map.
- Below the title bar the component of the material or map appear. By default, 3ds Max shows only those components that you can map.
- On the left side of each component a circular slot [marked as 1 in the right image of Figure F8] is available for input. You can use these sockets to wire maps to the node.
- On the right of the node, a circular slot [marked as 2 in the right image of Figure F8] that is used for the socket.

You can collapse a node to hide its slots. To do this, click on the minus sign [marked as 1 in Figure F9] available on the upper right corner of the node. To resize a node horizontally, drag the diagonal lines available on the bottom-right of the node [marked as 2 in Figure F9].

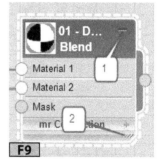

When you resize a node horizontally, it's easier to read the name of the slots. To change the preview icon size,double-click on the preview. To reduce the preview, double-click again. When a node's parameters are displayed in the **Parameter Editor**, 3ds Max shows a dashed border around the node in the active view [see Figure F10].

To create a new material, drag the material from the **Material/Map Browser** to the active view, 3ds Max places a node for the material in the active view. It is a good habit to change the name of the material immediately. It will make your life easier if you are working on a complex scene with tons of materials. To rename a material, RMB click on it and choose **Rename**. In the **Rename** dialog, change the name of the material and click **OK**. To change the properties of the material, double-click the node in the active view and then change the properties from the **Parameter Editor**.

Tip: Renaming materials
The name of a material can contain special characters, numbers, and spaces.

To get a material from the scene, click **Pick Material From Object** from the toolbar. Now, click on the object in a viewport to get the material. To apply a material to objects in the scene, drag the output socket of the node and then drop the wire on an object in the scene. As you drag the mouse in a viewport, a tooltip appears below the mouse pointer showing the name of the object. You can apply the material even if the object is not selected. If there is only one object selected in the scene, the material is immediately applied to that object. If there are more than one objects in the scene, 3ds Max prompts you to choose whether to apply the material to the single object or to the whole selection. You can also apply material to the selection by clicking **Assign Material To Selection** on the toolbar.

To make a copy of the existing material, drag the material from the **Material/Map Browser | Scene Materials** group (or any library) to the active View. The **Instance (Copy)** dialog appears. Select **Instance** or **Copy** from this dialog and click **OK**. To duplicate a node in the active view, select the node[s] that you want to duplicate and then drag the nodes with the **Shift** held down.

To select the objects onto which you have applied the same material, in the active view, select the node and then click **Select By Material** from the toolbar. 3ds Max opens the **Select Objects** dialog with the objects highlighted. Click **Select** to select the highlighted objects.

Selecting, Moving, and Laying Out Nodes

To select a node, ensure the **Select Tool** [hotkey **S**] is active, and then click on the node. To select multiple nodes, click on the nodes with the **Ctrl** held down. If you want to remove nodes from the selection, click on the nodes with **Alt** held down. To select all nodes, press **Ctrl+A**. To invert the selection, press **Ctrl+I**. To select none of the nodes, press **Ctrl+D**. To select children, press **Ctrl+C**. To select a node tree, press **Ctrl+T**. These functions are also accessible from the **Select** menu of the editor.

Note: Selected node
When a node is selected in the view, a white border appears around it. Also, the background including the title bar is darker. When node is not selected, the border appears gray and background is lighter.

Tip: Deselecting nodes
*To deselect nodes, click on the blank area of the view using the **Select Tool** .*

To move a node, drag it in the active view. To create clone of a node, drag it with the **Shift** held down. If you drag a node with **Ctrl+Shift** held down, 3ds Max clones the node and all its children. These methods also work on multiple selections.

If you want to move a node and its children, click **Move Children** ⯇ from the toolbar and drag a node. You can toggle this feature temporarily without clicking **Move Children** by moving the node with **Ctrl+Alt** held down. This feature can be accessed from the editor's **Options** menu. You can click the **Hide Unused** ⯇ option from the toolbar to hide the unused ports on the selected material.

The layout buttons on the toolbar allow you to arrange nodes in the active view. The **Layout All - Vertical** ⯇ and **Layout All - Horizontal** ⯇ buttons on the toolbar allow you to arrange nodes in an automatic layout along the vertical or horizontal axis in the active view. These options are also available in the editor's **View** menu. The **Layout Children** button allows you to automatically layout the children of the selected node.

If you turn on the **Show Shaded Material In Viewport** ⯇ from the toolbar for a material, a red diagonal shape appears on the node in the active view [see the left image in Figure F11]. The **Navigator** also shows a red diagonal shape to indicate this [see the middle image in Figure F11]. This shape also appears in the **Scene Materials** rollout of the **Material/Map Browser** [see the right image in Figure F11].

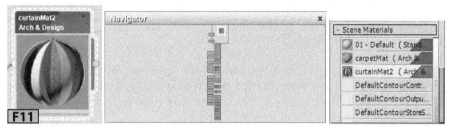

Previewing Materials

The **Preview** window [see Figure F12] of the editor allows you to visualize how material or map will appear in the scene. The main part of the window is a rendering of the material or map. You can resize this window like you resize any other window in 3ds max that is, by dragging its corners. Making a window larger helps you in visualizing the material, however, larger previews take longer to render. To open this window, RMB click on a node and then choose **Open Preview Window** from the popup menu.

To close a window, click **X** on the upper-right corner of the window. By default, a sphere is displayed as a sample geometry in the scene. If you want to change this geometry, choose **Cylinder** or **Box** from **RMB click** menu | **Preview Object Type** sub-menu. You can open any number of **Preview** windows in the editor. However, the drop-down available at the bottom of the **Preview** window allows you to switch the previews in a single window.

Caution: Preview window

*When open a new scene, the **Preview** window remains open, however, it may not correspond to any material. I recommend that you close all **Preview** windows before creating a new scene. The previews are not saved with the scene.*

When the **Auto** switch is on in the **Preview** window, 3ds Max automatically renders the preview again when you make any changes to the properties of a material or map. When this switch is off, the **Update** button becomes active. The render will be displayed only when you click **Update**. The **Show End Result** toggle available on the right of **Update** allows you to control when the **Preview** window displays a map. When off ![icon], the **Preview** window shows the map itself. When on, the **Preview** window shows the end result that is, the final result of the node.

Wiring Nodes

As you already know, wires are used to connect material or map components. To understand the wiring process, from the **Material/Map Browser | Materials** rollout | **General** rollout, drag **Standard** to the active view to create a **Standard** material node. Similarly, drag **Checker** from the **Material/Map Browser | Maps** rollout | **General** rollout to the active view to create a **Checker** node [see left image in Figure F13]. Click-drag the **Standard** material's **Diffuse Color** socket, a wire appears. Now, drop the wire on the output socket of the **Checker** node to make a connection [see the right image in Figure F13]. You can also connect in reverse. You can connect the output socket of the **Checker** node to the **Diffuse Color** slot of the **Standard** material.

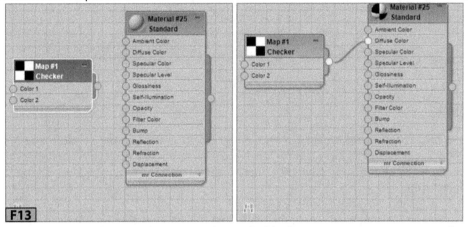

Now, drag and the **Standard** material's **Bump** socket to the blank area, a popup menu appears [see the left image in Figure F14], choose **Standard | Noise** from the menu to insert a **Noise** node and make connection between the **Noise** node and **Bump** socket of the **Standard** material [see the right image in Figure F14].

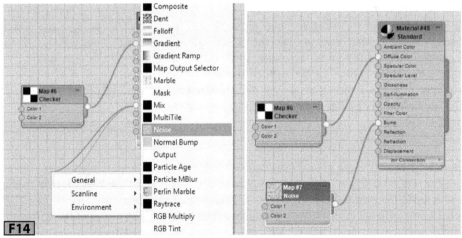

You can also connect a map directly to a socket without first dragging to the active view. To do this, drag the **Falloff** map from the **Material/Map Browser | Maps** rollout | **General** rollout to the **Reflection** socket of the **Standard** material. When the socket turns green, release the mouse to make the connection [see Figure

F15]. Another way to connect a node to a socket is that to double-click on a socket to open the **Material/Map Browser**. Now, select the desired map or material from the browser. You can also drag a wire on the title bar of a node. A popup menu appears [see Figure F16] that allows you to select component to wire.

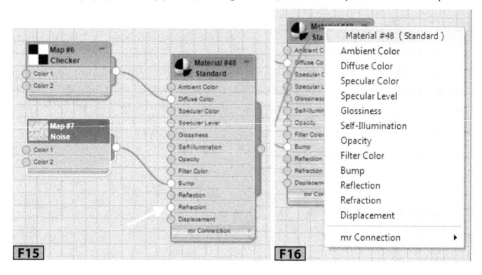

To delete a connection [wire], select the wire and then press **Delete**. The selected wire appears in white color. You can also drag away a wire from a socket where it has been connected to terminate the connection. To replace one map with another, drag from the new map's output socket to the output socket of the original map.

To insert a node into a connection, drag the node from the **Material/Map Browser** and then drop it on the wire. You can also drag from one of the node's input sockets to the wire to insert the node. If a node is lying on the active view and you want to insert it, drop the node on the wire with **Ctrl** held down. To disconnect an inserted node, drag the node and then press **Alt** while dragging.

When you RMB click on a wire, a popup menu appears [see Figure F17]. Choose **Change Material/Map Type** to open the **Material/Map Browser** and then choose a different type for the material or map. This option always affects the child node. The **Make Node Unique** option makes the child unique if the child node is instanced. The **Make Branch Unique** makes the child unique, as well as duplicates children of the child if the child node is instanced.

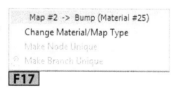

Views

The active view is the main area of the **Slate Material Editor** where all action takes place. The navigating the active view is similar to the navigating a scene in 3ds Max. To pan the view, drag with the MMB. If you drag with the MMB and **Ctrl+Alt** held down, 3ds max zooms the view. You can also zoom by scrolling the wheel. The navigational tools are also available at the bottom-right corner of the editor's interface.

Table 3 summarized these controls.

Table 3: The **Slate Material Editor** navigational controls		
Control	**Hotkey[s]**	**Menu**
Zoom percentage drop-down list	-	
Pan Tool	Ctrl+P	View	Pan Tool
Zoom Tool	Alt+Z	View	Zoom Tool
Zoom Region Tool	Ctrl+W	View	Zoom Region Tool
Zoom Extents	Ctrl+Alt+Z	View	Zoom Extents
Zoom Extents Selected	Z	Zoom Extents Selected
Pan to Selected	Alt+P	View	Pan to Selected

If you are working on a complex scene, you might face difficulties locating nodes in the active view. You can use the search function of the editor to locate the nodes in the scene. Make a habit of renaming the nodes as you create them so that you can find the nodes using their names. To search a node, click the **Search For Nodes** button available on the bottom-left corner of the active view, 3ds Max expands the search tool. Type the name of the node in the search field and press **Enter** to locate the node and zoom on the node in the active view.

By default, the **Navigator** window appears on the upper-right corner of the **Slate Material Editor**. This window is most useful when you have lots of material trees displayed in the active view. This window shows a map of the active view. The red rectangle in the navigator shows the border of the active view. If you drag the rectangle, 3ds max changes the focus of the view.

Named Views

If you are working on a complex scene, you can create named views to organize materials in a scene. You can create any number of views in the editor and then make one of them the active view. When you open the editor in a new scene, a single view is displayed with the name **View1**. To manage views, RMB click on one of the tab and then choose the desired options from the popup menu displayed [see Figure F18].

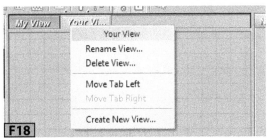

To cycle through the tabs, use the **Ctrl+Tab** hotkeys. You can also select a view from the drop-down available above the **Navigator**. To move a tree from one view to another, RMB click on the node and then choose **Move Tree to View | Name of the View** from the popup menu.

Summary
The unit covered the following topics:

- **Compact Material Editor**
- **Slate Material Editor**

Unit MT2 - General/Scanline Materials and Maps

The **General/Scanline Materials** materials are are non-photometric materials. Do not use these materials if you plan to create physically accurate lighting models. However, these materials are suitable for games, films, and animation. In this unit, we are going to look at the standard materials and maps.

In this unit, I'll describe the following:

- General/Scanline materials
- General maps

General/Scanline Materials

Let's explore the **Scanline** materials.

Standard Material

A surface having a single color reflects many other colors such as ambient, diffuse, and specular. The **Standard** materials use a four-color model to simulate the reflected colors from a surface. However, there may be variations depending on the shader you use. The **Ambient** color appears where surface is lit (the surface in the shadow) by the ambient light only. The **Diffuse** color appears on the surface when the lights falls directly on it. The term **Diffuse** is used because light is reflected in various directions. The **Specular** color appears in the highlights. Highlights are reflection of light sources on the surface.

Generally, shiny surfaces have specular highlights where the viewing angle is equal to the angle of incident. Metallic surfaces show another type of highlights called glancing highlights. The glancing highlights have a high angle of incidence. Some surfaces in the real-world are highly reflective. To model such surfaces, you can use a reflection map or use raytracing. The **Filter Color** is the color transmitted through an object. The **Filter Color** will only be visible, if **Opacity** is less than **100** percent.

The three color components blend at the edge of their respective regions. The **blend** of the **Diffuse** and **Ambient** components is controlled by the shader. However, you can control the blending by using the **Standard** material's highlight controls.

To create a **Standard** material, press **M** to open the **Slate Material Editor**. On the **Material Editor | Material /Map Browser | Materials | Scanline** rollout, double-click **Standard** to add a standard material node to the active view. Figure F1 shows the **Standard** material's interface. If you double-click on the material node, its attributes appear in various rollouts on the **Parameter Editor**. The controls on these rollouts change according to the shader type chosen from the **Shader Basic Parameters** rollout [see Figure F2].

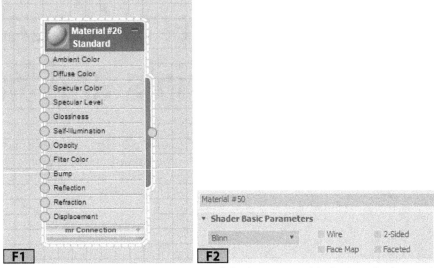

F1

F2

The controls in this rollout let you choose the type of shader to use with the **Standard** material. **Wire** lets you render the material in the wireframe mode [see Figure F3]. You can change the size of the wire using the **Size** control on the material's **Extended Parameters** rollout. Figure F4 shows the render with **Size** set to **2**. **2-Sided** allows you to make a 2-sided material. When you select this option, 3ds Max applies material to the both sides of the selected faces.

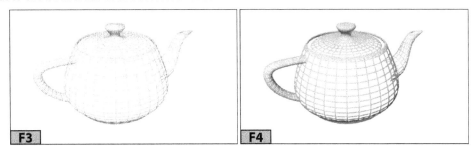

F3

F4

Note: One-sided faces

In 3ds Max, faces are one-sided. The front side is the side with the surface normals. The back side of the faces is invisible to the renderer. If you see this other side from the back, the faces will appear to be missing.

The **Face Map** control allows you to apply the material to the faces of the geometry. If material is a mapped material, it requires no mapping coordinates and automatically applied to each face. Figures F5 and F6 show the render with the **Face Map** switch is in off and on states, respectively. The **Faceted** control renders each face of the surface as if it were flat [see Figure F7].

Tip: Rendering both sides of a face

*There are two ways to render both sides of a face. Either you can turn on **Force 2-Sided** in the **Render Setup** dialog | **Common** panel | **Options** section or apply a two sided material to the faces.*

The **Shader** drop-down located at the extreme left of the rollout lets you choose a shader for the material.

F5 **F6** **F7**

Here's is the quick rundown to the various material shaders:

Phong Shader

You use this shader to produce realistic highlights for shiny, and regular surfaces. This shader produces strong circular highlights. This shader can accurately render bump, opacity, shininess, specular, and reflection maps. When you select the **Phong** shader, the **Phong Shader Parameters** rollout appears in the material's **Parameter Editor** [see Figure F8].

Phong Shader Parameters Rollout

The controls in this rollout, let you set the color of the material, shininess, and transparency of the material. The **Ambient**, **Diffuse**, and **Specular** controls let you set the colors for ambient, diffuse, and specular color components, respectively. To change a color component, click on the color swatch and then use the **Color Selector** to change the values of the color component. You can also copy one color component to another by dragging the source color swatch to the target color swatch. In the **Copy or Swap Colors** dialog that appears, click **Swap**, or **Copy** button. Click **Cancel** to cancel the operation. You can lock or unlock two color components using the **Lock** button [see Figure F9].

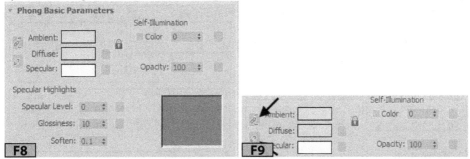

F8 **F9**

The buttons located on the right of color swatches can be used to apply texture maps to the respective color components. On clicking these buttons, the **Material/Map Browser** appears that allows you to select a map for the color component. If you want to apply different maps to the **Ambient** and **Diffuse** components, click on the **Lock** button located to the right of these components [see Figure F10].

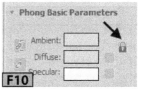

F10

Self-Illumination Group: You can use the controls in this group to make the material self-illuminated. The illusion of self-illumination is created by replacing shadows with the diffuse color. There are two ways to enable self-illumination in 3ds Max. Either you can turn on the switch located in this group and use a self-illumination color or use the spinner.

Note: Self-illuminated materials
Self-illuminated materials do not show shadows cast onto them. Also, they are unaffected by the lights in the scene.

Opacity Group: You can use the controls in this group, to make a material opaque, transparent, or translucent. To change the opacity of the material, change opacity to a value less than 100%. If you want to use a map for controlling opacity, click **Opacity** map button.

Specular Highlight Group: Phong, Blinn, and **Oren-Nayar-Blinn** shaders produce circular highlights and share same highlight controls. **Blinn** and **Oren-Nayar-Blinn** shaders produce soft and round highlights than the **Phong** shader. You can use the **Specular Level** control to increase or decrease the strength of a highlight. As you change the value for this control, the **Highlight** curve and the highlight in the preview changes. The shape of this curve affects the blending between the specular and diffuse color components of the material. If the curve is steeper, there will be less blending and the edge of the specular highlight will be sharper. To increase or decrease the size of the highlight, change the value for **Glossiness**. **Soften** softens the specular highlights especially those formed by the glancing light.

Extended Parameters Rollout

The **Extender Parameters** rollout [see Figure F11] is same for all shaders except **Strauss** and **Translucent** shaders. The controls in this rollout allow you to control the transparency and reflection settings. Also, it has controls for adjusting the wireframe rendering.

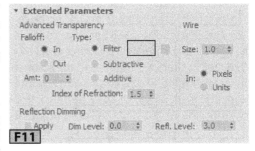

Advanced Transparency Group: These controls do not appear for the **Translucent** shader. **Falloff** allows you to set the falloff and its extent. **In** increases transparency toward the inside of the object (like glass bottle) whereas **Out** increases transparency toward the outside of the object (like clouds). **Amt** lets you adjust the amount of transparency at the outside or inside extreme.

The **Type** controls let you specify how transparency is applied. The **Filter** color swatch computes a filter color that it multiplies with the color behind the transparent surface. The **Subtractive** option subtracts from the color behind the transparent surface. The **Additive** option adds to the color behind the transparent surface.

Index of Refraction allows you to set the index of refraction used by refraction map and raytracing.

Reflection Dimming group: This group does not appear for the **Strauss** shader. These controls dim the reflection in shadow. Tun on the **Apply** switch to enable reflection dimming. **Dim Level** controls the amount of dimming that takes place in shadow. **Refl. Level** affects the intensity of the reflection that is not in shadow.

SuperSampling Rollout

The **SuperSampling** rollout [see Figure F12] is used by the **Architectural, Raytrace, Standard**, and **Ink 'n Paint** materials to improve the quality of the rendered image. It performs an additional antialiasing pass on the material thus resulting in more render time. By default, a single **SuperSampling** method is applied to all materials in the scene.

Note: Super Sampling
*The **Super Sampling** method is ignored by **mental ray** as it has its own sampling algorithm.*

Maps Rollout: The **Maps** rollout [see Figure F13] is available for all materials. The controls in this rollout allow you to assign maps to various components of the material. To assign map to a component, click a map button. Now, choose the desired map option from the **Material/Map Browser** that opens.

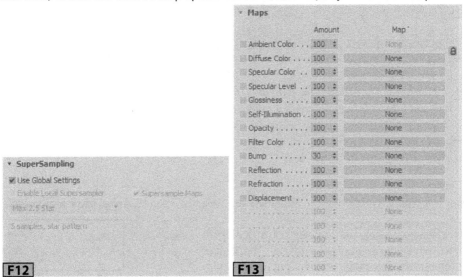

F12   F13

Blinn Shader

This is the default shader. It produces rounder, softer highlights than the **Phong** shader. The **Blinn** and **Phong** shaders have the same basic parameters.

Metal Shader

You can use the **Metal** shader to create realistic-looking metallic surfaces and a variety of organic-looking materials. The metal material calculates their specular color automatically. The output specular color depends on the diffuse color of the material and the color of the light.

This shader produces distinctive highlights. Like the **Phong** shader, **Specular Level** still controls intensity. However, **Glossiness** affects both the intensity and size of the specular highlights. Figure F14 shows the controls in **Metal Basic Parameters** rollout.

Oren-Nayar-Blinn Shader

This shader is a variant of the **Blinn** shader and can be used to model matte surfaces such as fabric. It has two additional controls to model a surface with the matte look: **Diffuse Level** and **Roughness**.

[**Oren-Nayar-Blinn Basic Parameters rollout | Advanced Diffuse Group**]: **Diffuse Level** controls [see Figure F15] the brightness of the diffuse component of the material. It allows you to make the material lighter or darker. **Roughness** allows you to control the rate at which the diffuse component blends into the ambient component.

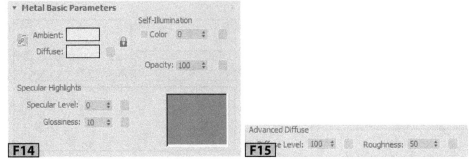

Note: The Roughnesss Parameter

The **Roughness** *parameter is available only with the* **Oren-Nayar-Blinn** *and* **Multi-Level** *shaders, and with the* **Arch & Design** *and* **Physical** *materials* (**mental ray**).

Note: Diffuse Level control

The **Blinn**, **Metal**, **Phong**, *and* **Strauss** *shaders do not have the* **Diffuse Level** *control.*

Strauss Shader

This shader is a simpler version of the **Metal** shader. It can be used to model the metallic surfaces.

Strauss Basic Parameters Rollout: The **Color** control [see Figure F16] lets you specify the color of the material. The **Strauss** shader automatically calculates the ambient and specular color components. **Glossiness** controls the size and intensity of the specular highlights. On increasing the value for this control, the highlight gets smaller and the material appears shiner. The **Metalness** control adjust the

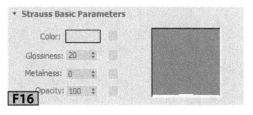

metalness of the surface. The effect of this control is more prominent when you increase the **Glossiness** value. **Opacity** sets the transparency of the material.

Anisotropic Shader

You can use this shader to create surfaces with elliptical, anisotropic highlights. This shader is suitable for modeling hair, glass, or brushed metal. The **Diffuse Level** controls are similar to that of the **Oren-Nayar-Blinn** shading controls, and basic parameters controls are similar to that of the **Blinn** or **Phong** shading, except the **Specular Highlights** parameters.

Anisotropic Basic Parameters Rollout | Specular Highlight Group: The **Specular Level** [Figure F17] control sets the intensity of the specular highlights. On increasing the value for this control, the highlight goes brighter. **Glossiness** controls the size of the specular highlights. The **Anisotropy** controls the anisotropy or shape of the highlight. **Orientation** controls the orientation of the highlight. This value is measured in degrees.

Multi-Layer Shader

This shader is similar to the **Anisotropic** shader. However, it allows you to layer two sets of specular highlights. The highlights are layered that allows you to create complex highlights. Figure F18 shows the two specular layers in the **Multi-Layer Basic Parameters** rollout.

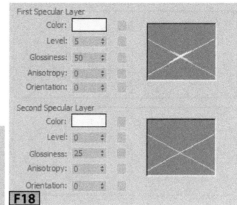

Translucent Shader

This shader is similar to the **Blinn** shader but allows you set the translucency of the material. A translucent object not only allows light to pass through but it also scatters light within.

Translucent Basic Parameters Rollout | Translucency Group: The **Translucent Clr** control [see Figure F19] sets the translucency color that is the color of the light scattered within the material. This color is different from the **Filter** color which

is the color transmitted through transparent or semi-transparent material such as glass. The **Opacity** control sets the opacity or transparency of the material.

Note: The mental ray renderer

The **mental ray** *renderer is used in hands-on-exercises of this book.*

Raytrace Material

This material is an advanced surface-shading material. It supports the same diffuse surface shading that a **Standard** material supports.

However, it also supports fog, color density, translucency, fluorescence, and other special effects. This material is capable of creating fully raytraced reflections and refractions. Figure F20 shows the **Raytrace** material's interface.

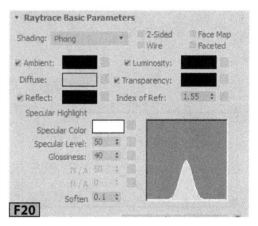

Architectural Material

The properties of this material [see Figure F21] create realistic looking images when used with Photometric lights and Radiosity. Therefore, you should use this material when you are looking for high level of accuracy. If you don't need the high detail this material produces, use the Standard material or any other material.

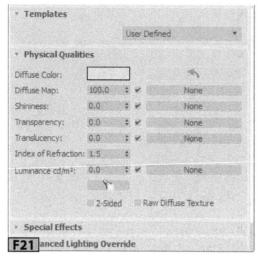

F21 anced Lighting Override

When you create a new **Architectural** material, you can choose from a wide variety of templates that are built into this material. You can use these templates as starting point for the shading model you wish to create. You can choose template from the drop-down available in the **Templates** rollout.

Advanced Lighting Override Material

You can use this material to directly control the radiosity properties of a material. You can use this material directly. It is a always a supplement to the base material [see Figure F22]. This material has no effect on the ordinary renderings. It is used with Radiosity and Light Tracing solutions.

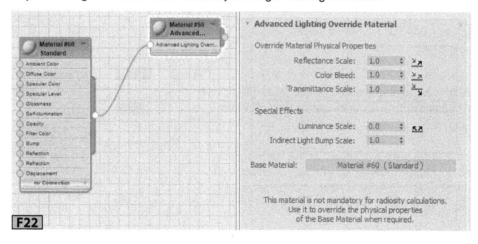

F22

This material has two primary usages:

- Adjusting properties of a material used in a Radiosity and Light Tracing solutions.
- Contributing energy to the Radiosity solution with self-illuminating objects.

Caution: The mental ray renderer
*The **mental ray** renderer does not support this material.*

General Materials

Let's explore the **General** materials.

Blend Material

The **Blend** material allows you to mix two materials on a single side of the surface. You can use the **Mix Amount** parameter [see Figure F23] to control the way two materials are blended together. You can also animate this control. The **Material 1** and **Material 2** controls let you assign the two materials to be blended. You can also use the corresponding switches to turn material on or off. The **Interactive** option specifies which of the materials or mask map will be displayed in the viewport by the interactive renderer.

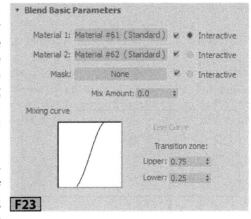

The **Mask** control lets you assign a map as mask. The lighter and darker areas on the mask map control the degree of blending. The lighter areas displays more of the **Material 1** whereas the darker areas show more of **Material 2**. The **Mix Amount** controls the proportion of blend in degrees. A value of **0** means only **Material 1** will be visible on the surface whereas a value of **100** means **Material 2** will be visible on the surface.

When you assign a mask map for blending, you can use the mixing curve to affect the blending. You can use the controls in the **Transition Zone** group to adjust the level of the **Upper** and **Lower** limits.

Note: Interactive renderer and Blend material
Only one map can be displayed in the viewports when using the interactive renderer.

Note: Blend Material and Noise Map
*The **Mix Amount** control is not available when you use mask to blend the material. Using a **Noise** map as mixing map can produce naturally looking surfaces.*

Double Sided Material

The **Double Sided** material lets you assign two different materials to the front and back surface of an object. The **Facing Material** and **Back Material** controls [see Figure F24] allow you to specify the material for the front and back faces, respectively. The **Translucency** control allows you to blend the two materials. There will be no blending of the materials if **Translucency** is set to **0**. At a value of **100**, the outer material will be visible on the inner faces and inner material will be visible on the outer faces.

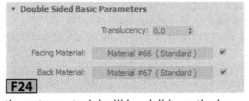

Composite Material

This material can be used to composite up to ten materials. The materials are composited from top to bottom. The maps can be combined using additive opacity, subtractive opacity, or using an amount value. The **Base Material** control [see Figure F25] allows you to set the base material. The default base material is the **Standard** material.

The **Mat.1** to **Mat.9** controls are used to specify the material that you want to composite. Each material control has an array of buttons called **ASM** buttons. These buttons control how the material is composited. The **A** button allows you to use the additive opacity.

The colors in the materials are summed based on the opacity. The **S** button allows you to use the subtractive opacity. The **M** button is used to mix the materials using a value. You can enter the value in the spinner located next to the **M** button. When the **M** button is active, amount ranges from **0** to **100**. When amount is **0**, no compositing happens and the material below is not visible. If the amount is **100**, the material below is visible.

Tip: Composite Material v Composite Map
*If you want to achieve a result by combining maps instead of combining materials, use the **Composite** map that provides greater control.*

Note: Overloaded compositing
*For additive and subtractive compositing, the amount can range from **0** to **200**. When the amount is greater than **100**, the compositing is overloaded. As a result, the transparent area of the material becomes more opaque.*

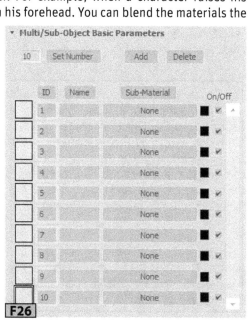

Morpher Material

The **Morpher** material is used with the **Morpher** modifier. For example, when a character raises his eyebrows, you can use this material to display wrinkles on his forehead. You can blend the materials the same way you morph the geometry using the channel spinners of the **Morpher** modifier.

Multi/Sub-Object Material

The **Multi/Sub-Object** material allows you to assign materials at the sub-object level. The number field [see Figure F26] shows the number of sub-materials contained in the **Multi/Sub-Object** material. You can use the **Set Number** button to set the number of sub-materials that make up the material. The **Add** button allows you to a new sub-material to the list. Use the **Delete** button to remove currently chosen sub-material from the list. The **ID**, **Name**, and **Sub-Material** controls allow you to sort the list based on the material id, name, and sub-material, respectively.

To assign materials to the sub-objects, select the object and assign the **Multi/sub-Object** material to it. Apply a **Mesh Select** modifier to the object. Activate the **Face** sub-object level. Now, select the faces to which you will assign the material. Apply a **Material Modifier** and then set the material ID value to the number of the sub-material you need to assign.

Shellac Material

Shellac material allows you to mix two materials by superimposing one over the other. The superimposed material is known as the **Shellac** material. The **Base Material** control [Figure F27] lets you choose or edit the base sub-material. The **Shellac Material** control lets you choose or edit the **Shellac** material. The **Shellac Color Blend** control adjusts the amount of color mixing. The default value for this control is **0**. Hence, the **Shellac** material has

no effect on the surface. There is no upper limit for this control. Higher values overload the colors of the **Shellac** material. You can also animate this parameter.

Top/Bottom Material

This material lets you assign two different materials to the top and bottom portions of an object. You can also blend the two materials. The top faces of an object are those faces whose normals point up. The bottom faces have the normals down. You can control the boundary between the top and bottom using the controls available in the **Coordinates** group [see Figure F28].

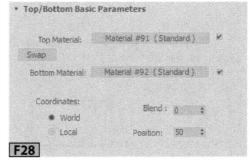

The **World** option lets you specify the direction according to the world coordinates of the scene. If you rotate the object, the boundary between the top and bottom faces remains in place. The **Local** option allows you to control the direction using the local coordinate system.

You can specify the top and bottom materials using the **Top** and **Bottom** controls, respectively. The **Swap** button allows you to swap the material. You can blend the edge between the top and bottom materials using the **Blend** control. The value for this control ranges from **0** to **1**. If you set **Blend** to **0**, there will be a sharp line between the top and bottom materials. At **100**, the two materials tint each other.

The **Position** control allows you to specify the location where the division between the two materials will occur. The value for this control ranges from **0** to **1**. If you set **Position** to **0**, only top material will be displayed. At **100**, only bottom material will be displayed.

Matte/Shadow Material

The **Matte Shadow** material is used to make whole objects or any set of faces into matte objects. The matte objects reveal the background color or the environment map. A matte object is invisible but it blocks any geometry behind it however it does not block the background. The matte objects can also receive shadows. The shadows cast on the matte object are applied to the alpha channel. To properly generate shadows on a matte object, turn off **Opaque Alpha** and then turn on **Affect Alpha**.

Ink 'n Paint Material

The **Ink 'n Paint** material is used to create cartoons effects. This material produces shading with inked borders.

DirectX Shader Material

It is a special material that allows you to shade objects in the viewport using DirectX (Direct3D) shaders. When you use this material, materials in the viewport more accurately represent how they will look on some other software or hardware device.

Tip: Quicksilver hardware renderer
*You can use the **Quicksilver hardware renderer** to render **DirectX Shader** materials.*

XRef Material

This material lets you use a material applied to an object in another 3ds Max scene file. This material is typically used with the XRef objects. You can also use the **Override Material** rollout to assign a local material to the XRef'd object.

Physical Material

Physical material allows you to model shading effects of the real-world materials with ease. This material is the layered material that gives you ability to efficiently use the physically-based workflows. This material is compatible with **ART** and **mental ray** renderers.

General/Scanline Maps

Maps allow you to improve the appearance of the materials. They also help you to enhance the realism of the materials. You can use maps in a variety of ways, you can use them to create environments, to create image planes for modeling, to create projections from light, and so forth. You can use the **Material/ Map Browser** to load a map or create a map of a particular type. A map can be used to design different elements of a material such as reflection, refraction, bump, and so forth.

Maps and Mapping Coordinates

When you apply a map to any object, the object must have mapping coordinates applied. These coordinates are specified in terms of UVW axes local to the object. Most of the objects in 3ds Max have the **Generate Mapping Coordinates** option. When on, 3ds Max generates default mapping coordinates.

UVW Mapping Coordinate Channels

Each object in 3ds Max can have **99** UVW mapping coordinates. The default mapping is always assigned the number **1**. The **UVW Map** modifier can send coordinates to any of these **99** channels.

3ds Max gives you ability to generate the mapping coordinates in different ways:

- The **Generate Mapping Coords** option is available for most of the primitives. This option provides a projection appropriate to the shape of the object type.
- Apply the **Unwrap UVW** modifier. This modifier comes with some useful tools that you can use to edit mapping coordinates.
- Apply the **UVW Map** modifier. This modifier allows you to set a projection type from several projection types it provides.

Here's the quick rundown to the projection types:

- Box projection: It places a duplicate of the map image on each of the six sides of a box.

- Cylindrical projection: This wraps the image around the sides of the object. The duplicate images are also projected onto the end caps.

- Spherical projection: This projection type wraps the map image around a sphere and gather the image at the top and bottom.

- Shrink-wrap projection: This type is like the spherical projection but creates one singularity instead of two.

- Use special mapping coordinates. For example, the **Loft** object provides built-in mapping coordinates.
- Use a **Surface Mapper** modifier. This modifier uses a map assigned to a NURBS surface and projects it onto the object(s).

Here's quick rundown to the cases when you can apply a map and you don't need mapping coordinates:

- Reflection, Refraction, and Environment maps.
- 3D Procedural maps: **Noise** and **Marble**.
- Face-mapped materials.

Tip: UVW Remove utility
*The **UVW Remove** utility removes mapping coordinates or materials from the currently selected objects. The path to the utility is as follows: **Utilities** panel | **Utilities** rollout | **More** button | **Utilities** dialog | **UVW Remove**. You can also remove material from objects using the **UVW Remove** utility.*

Real-World Mapping
The real-world mapping is an alternative mapping method that you can use in 3ds Max. This type of mapping considers the correct scaling of the texture mapped materials applied to the geometry in the scene.

Note: Autodesk Materials
Autodesk materials require you to use the real-world mapping.

In order to apply the real-world mapping correctly, two requirements must be met. First, the correct style of UV texture coordinates must be assigned to the geometry. In other words, the size of the UV space should correspond to the size of the geometry. To address this issue, the **Real-World Map Size** switch is added to the many rollouts in 3ds Max [see Figure F29].

The second requirement is available in the **Coordinates** rollout of the **Material Edito**, the **Use Real-World Scale** switch. When this switch is on, **U/V** changes to **Width/Height** and **Tiling** changes to **Size** [see Figure F30].

Note: Real–world Mapping
The real–world mapping is off in 3ds Max, by default.

Tip: Real–World Map Size check box
*You can turn on **Real–World Map Size** by default from the **Preferences** dialog by using the **Use Real–World Texture Coordinates** switch. This option is available in the **Texture Coordinates** section of the **General** panel.*

Output Rollout

The options in this rollout [see Figure F31] are responsible for setting the internal parameters of a map. These options can be used to determine the rendered appearance of the map. Most of the controls on this rollout are for the color output.

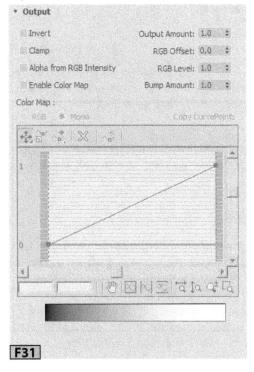

Note: Output Rollout
*These controls do not affect the bump maps except the **Invert** toggle, which reverses the direction of the bumps and bump amount.*

MT2-14   Unit MT2 - General/Scanline Materials and Maps

2D Maps

The 2D maps are two-dimensional images that are mapped to the surface of the geometric objects. You can also use them to create environment maps. The **Bitmap** is the simplest type 2D maps. 3ds Max also allows you to create 2D maps procedurally.

Coordinates Rollout

The **Coordinates** rollout shown in Figure F30 allows you to adjust coordinate parameters to move a map relative to the surface of the object. This rollout also allows you to set tiling and mirroring of the texture pattern. The repetition of the texture pattern on the surface of an object is known as tiling. The mirroring is a form of tiling in which 3ds Max repeats the map and then flips the repeated map.

In this rollout, there are two options that you can use to control the mapping type. These options are **Texture** and **Environ**. The **Texture** type applies texture as a map to the surface. The **Environ** type uses map as an environment map. For both of these options, you can select the types of coordinates from the **Mapping** drop-down.

Here's the list of options available in the **Mapping** drop-down:

- **Explicit Map Channel:** It uses any map channel from **1** to **99**. When you select this option, **Map Channel** becomes active.
- **Vertex Color Channel:** This option uses assigned vertex colors as a channel.
- **Planar from Object XYZ:** This option uses planar mapping based on the object's local coordinates.
- **Planar from World XYZ:** This option uses planar mapping based on the scene's world coordinates.
- **Spherical Environment/Cylindrical Environment/Shrink-wrap Environment:** These options project the map into the scene as if it were mapped to an invisible object in the background.
- **Screen:** This option projects a map as a flat backdrop in the scene.

Noise Rollout

You can add a random noise to the appearance of the material using the parameters available in this rollout [see Figure F32]. These parameters modify the mapping of pixels by applying a fractal noise function.

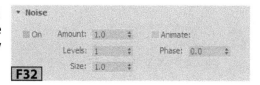

Bitmap

This map is the simplest type of map available in 3ds Max. This map is useful for creating many type of materials from wood to skin. If you want to create an animated material, you can use an animation or video file with this map. When you select this map, the **Select Bitmap Image File** dialog opens. Navigate to the location where the bitmap file is stored and then click **Open** to select the file.

Tip: Bitmap and Windows Explorer
You can also create a bitmap node by dragging a supported bitmap file from ***Windows Explorer*** *to the* ***Slate Material Editor.***

Tip: Viewport Canvas
The ***Viewport Canvas*** *feature allows you create a bitmap on the fly by painting directly onto the surface of the object. To open the canvas, choose* ***Viewport Canvas*** *from the* ***Tools*** *menu.*

Checker Map

This map is a procedural texture that applies a two-color checkerboard pattern [see Figure F33]. The default colors used to produce the pattern are black and white. You can also change these colors with map and it's true for all color components of the other maps.

Camera Map Per Pixel Map

This map allows you to project a map from the direction of a particular camera. It is useful when you are working on a matte painting. Figure F34 shows the **Marble** map projected on the teapot using the camera [see Figure F35]. Figure F36 shows the node network.

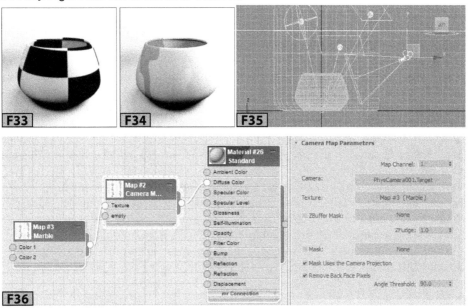

Note: Two maps with the sane name
If a map with the same name exists in two places, only one map is loaded to save the loading time. If you have two maps with different contents but with the same name, only the first map encountered by 3ds Max appears in the scene.

Tip: Swapping Colors
*You can swap colors by dragging one color swatch over another and then choosing **Swap** from the popup menu.*

Warning: Camera Map Per Pixel Map
This map cannot be used with the animated objects or animated textures.

Gradient Map

This map type allows you to create a gradient that shades from one color to another. Figure F37 shows the shift from one color to another. The red, green, and blue colors are used for the gradient. Figure F38 shows the result when the fractal noise is applied to the gradient. Figure F39 shows the node network.

Gradient Ramp Map

This map is similar to the **Gradient** map. Like the **Gradient** map, it shades from one color to another, however, you can use any number of colors [see Figure F40]. Also, you have additional controls to create a complex customized ramp. Figure F41 shows the node network used to produce the result shown in Figure F40.

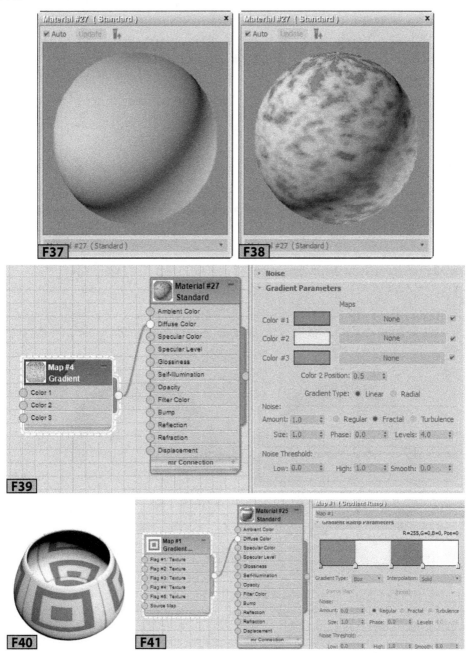

F37

F38

F39

F40

F41

Normal Bump Map

This map allows you to connect a texture-baked normal map to a material. Figure F42 shows the bump on the surface created using the **Normal Bump** map. Figure F43 shows the node network.

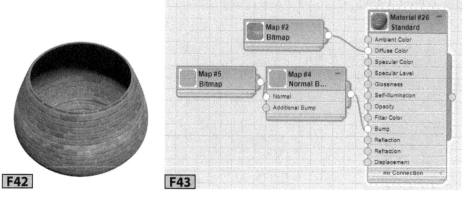

F42

F43

Substance Map

This map is used with the **Substance** parametric textures. These textures are resolution-independent 2D textures and use less memory. Therefore, they are useful for exporting to the game engines via the **Algorithmic Substance Air** middleware.

Swirl Map

This map is 2D procedural map that can be used to simulate swirls [see Figure F44].

Tiles Map

You can use this map to create a brick or stacked tiling of colors or maps. A number of commonly used architectural brick patterns are available with this map. Figure F45 shows render with the **English Bond** type applied.

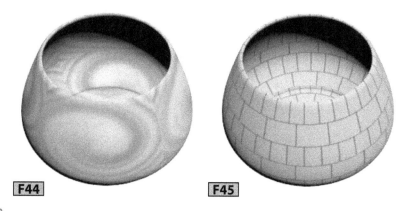

F44

F45

Vector Map

Using this map, you can apply a vector-based graphics, including animation as textures. You can also use **AutoCAD Pattern** (PAT) files, **Adobe Illustrator** (AI) files, **Portable Document** (PDF) files, and **Scalable Vector Graphics** (SVG) files [see Figure 46].

Vector Displacement Map

This map allows you to displace the meshes in three directions whereas the traditional method permits displacement only along the surface normals.

3D Maps

3D maps are patterns generated by 3ds Max in 3D space. Let's have a look at various 3D maps.

Cellular Map

You can use this map to generate a variety of visual effects such as mosaic tiling, pebbled surfaces, and even ocean surfaces [see Figure F47].

Dent Map

This map generated a procedural map using a fractal noise algorithm. The effect that this produces depends on the map type chosen.

Falloff Map

The **Falloff** map generates a value from white to black based on the angular falloff of the face normals. Figure F48 shows the **Falloff** map applied to the geometry with the **Falloff** type set to **Fresnel**.

Marble Map

You can use this map to create a marble texture with the colored veins against [see Figure F49] a color background.

Noise Map

This map allows to create a noise map that creates the random perturbation of a surface based on the interaction of two colors or materials. Figure F50 shows the **Noise** map with the **Noise Type** set to **Fractal**.

Particle Age Map

This map is used with the particle systems. This map changes the color of the particles based on their age.

Particle MBlur Map

This map can be used to alter the opacity of the leading and trailing ends of particles based on their rate of motion.

Perlin Marble Map

This map is like the **Marble** map. However, it generates a marble pattern using the **Perlin Turbulence** algorithm.

Smoke Map

You can use this map [see Figure F51] to create animated opacity maps to simulate the effects of smoke in a beam of light, or other cloudy, flowing effects.

F49   F50   F51

Speckle Map
This map [see Figure F52] can be used to create granite-like and other patterned surfaces.

Splat Map
This map can be used to create patterns similar to the spattered paint [see Figure F53].

Stucco Map
You can use this map [see Figure F54] as a bump to create the effect like a stuccoed surface.

F52   F53   F54

Waves Map
You can use this map as both bump or diffuse map [see Figure F55]. This map is used to create watery or wavy effects.

Wood Map
This map creates a wavy grain like wood pattern [see Figure F56]. You can control the direction, thickness, and complexity of the grain.

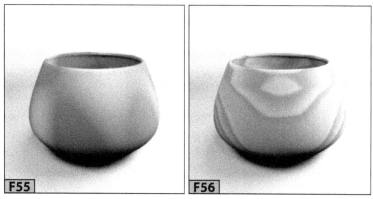

F55   F56

Compositor Maps

These maps are specifically designed for compositing colors and maps. Let's have a look at these maps.

Composite Map

You can use this map to layer other maps atop each other using the alpha channel and other methods.

Mask Map

This map can be used to view one material through another on the surface.

Mix Map

With this map, you can combine two colors or materials on a single side of the surface. You can also animate the **Mix Amount** parameter to control how two maps are blended together over time.

RGB Multiply Map

This map combines two maps by multiplying their RGB values. This map is generally used as a **Bump** map.

Color Modifiers Maps

These maps change the color of the pixels in a material. Let's have a look:

Color Correction Map

This map is allows you to modify color of a map using various tools. This map uses a stack-based method.

Output Map

You can use this map to apply output settings to the procedural maps such as **Checker** or **Marble**. These maps don't have the output settings.

RGB Tint Map

This map adjusts the three color channels in an image.

Vertex Color Map

In 3ds Max, you can assign vertex colors using the **VertexPaint** modifier, the **Assign Vertex Colors** utility, or the vertex controls for an editable mesh, editable patch, or editable poly. This map makes any vertex coloring applied to an object available for rendering.

Reflection and Refraction Maps

These maps are used to create reflections and refractions. Here's is a quick rundown.

Flat Mirror Map

This map produces a material that reflects surroundings when it is applied to the co-planer faces. It is assigned to the **Reflection** map of the material.

Raytrace Map

This map allows you to create fully raytraced reflections and refractions. The reflections/refractions generated by this map are more accurate than the **Reflect/Refract** map.

Reflect/Refract Map

You can use this map to create a reflective or refractive surface. To create reflection, assign this map type to the reflection map. To create refraction, apply it to the **Refraction** map.

Thin Wall Refraction Map

This map can be used to simulate a surface as if it part of a surface through a plate of glass.

Other Maps

In 2017 version of 3ds Max, Autodesk has introduced some new maps. Here's is a quick rundown.

Shape Map

You can use this map to create resolution independent graphical textures that you can animate. This map uses splines to apply textures to the selected object. The results can be fully animated. You can set outlines, fill colors as well as the map boundaries. You can change the shape of the spline even after applying it to the object in the scene. Also, all adjustment to the shape can be keyframed as a result you can animate the textures. The functioning of this map is demonstrated in an hands-on exercise later in the unit.

Text Map

Like splines, you can also create textures using text. You can create creative textures using the **Text** map and all adjustments can be animated. The functioning of this map is demonstrated in an hands-on exercise later in the unit.

TextureObjMask

This texture map allows you to control the textures using a primitive control object [plane, box, or sphere]. You can use the box or sphere primitive to control inside/outside color. The plan primitive allows you to control above/below color. The functioning of this map is demonstrated in an hands-on exercise later in the unit.

Color Map

This map allows you to create solid color swatches and bitmaps. You can easily create and instance solid color swatches that allows you to maintain consistency and accuracy of color choices. You can also use a bitmap as an input and adjust gamma and gain.

Combustion

You can use this map to interactively create maps using Autodesk Combustion and 3ds Max simultaneously. When you paint a map in combustion the material automatically updated in 3ds Max [material editor and shaded viewports].

Caution: Combustion

This map works only if Autodesk Combustion is installed on your system. 3ds Max is only available for Windows, as a result, you can not use this map on a Macintosh system.

Map Output Selector

This map is used with the multi-output map such as Substance. It tells 3ds Max which output to use. This map is automatically inserted when you assign an output of multi-output Substance map to input of a material.

MultiTile

This texture allows you to implement support for UDIM, Z-Brush, and Mudbox compaitble multi-tile textures. ZBrush is the default value.

Hands-on Exercises

From the **Application** menu, choose **Manage | Set Project Folder** to open the **Browse for Folder** dialog. Navigate to the folder where you want to save the files and then click **Make New Folder**. Create the new folder with the name **unit-mt2** and click **OK** to create the project directory.

Exercise 1: Creating the Gold Material

In this exercise, we are going to create the gold material.

The following table summarizes the exercise.

Table E1: Creating the gold material	
Topics in this section:	• Getting Ready • Creating the Gold Material
Skill Level	Beginner
Project Folder	**unit-mt2**
Start File	**umt2-hoe1-1to13-start.max**
Final Exercise File	**umt2-hoe1-end.max**
Time to Complete	10 Minutes

Getting Ready

Open the **umt2-hoe1-1to13-start.max** file in 3ds Max.

Creating the Gold Material

Press M to open the **Slate Material Editor**. On the **Material/Map Browser | Materials | General** rollout, drag the **Standard** material to the active view. Rename the material as **goldMat**. Apply the material to **geo1, geo2**, and **geo3**. Save the scene as **umt2-hoe1-end.max**. On the **Parameter Editor | goldMat | Shader Basic Parameters** rollout, choose **Multi-Layer** from the drop-down. On the **Multi-Layer Basic Parameters** rollout, set **Diffuse** to **RGB [148, 70, 0]** and then set **Diffuse Level** to **25**. Take a test render [see Figure E1].

Now, we will add specularity and reflection to add the detail. On the **First Specular Layer** section, set **Color** to **RGB [247, 227, 10]**. Set **Level** to **114**, **Glossiness** to **32**, **Anisotropy** to **82**, and **Orientation** to **90**. On the **Second Specular Layer** section, set **Color** to **RGB [192, 77, 8]**. Set **Level** to **114**, **Glossiness** to **32**, **Anisotropy** to **82**, and **Orientation** to **90**. On the **Maps** rollout, click **Reflection** map button. On the **Material/Map Browser** that appears, double-click **Falloff**.

On the **Parameter Editor | Falloff | Falloff Parameters** rollout, click the **Swap Color/Maps** button. Also, set **Falloff Type** to **Fresnel**. Click white swatch map button and then on the **Material/Map Browser** that appears, double-click **Raytrace** in the **General** rollout. On the **Parameter Editor | Raytrace | Raytracer Parameters** rollout, select **Reflection** from the **Trace Mode** section. Take a test render [see Figure E2].

On the **Falloff | Mix Curve** rollout, RMB click on the first point and then choose **Bezier-Corner** from the contextual menu [see Figure E3]. Similarly, convert second point to **Bezier-Corner** and change the shape of the curve as shown in Figure E4. Now, take a render to view the final result [see Figure E5].

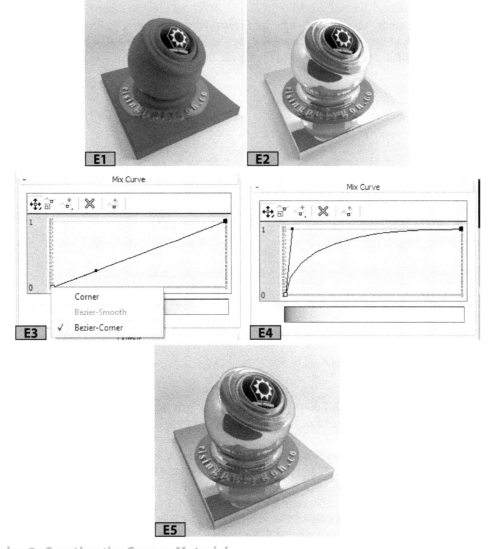

Exercise 2: Creating the Copper Material

In this exercise, we are going to create the copper material.

The following table summarizes the exercise.

Table E2: Creating the copper material	
Topics in this section:	• Getting Ready • Creating the Copper Material
Skill Level	Beginner
Project Folder	**unit-mt2**

Start File	umt2-hoe1-end.max
Final Exercise File	umt2-hoe2-end.max
Time to Complete	10 Minutes

Getting Ready

Make sure the **umt2-hoe1-end.max** file that you created in Hands-on Exercise 1 is open in 3ds Max.

Creating the Copper Material

Press M to open the **Slate Material Editor**, if not already open. Create a copy of the **goldMat** node by shift dragging it [see Figure E1].

Rename the node as **copperMat** and then apply it to **geo1**, **geo2**, and **geo3**. Save the scene as **umt2-hoe2-end.max**.

On the **Multi-Layer Basic Parameters** rollout, set **Diffuse** to **RGB [88, 28, 9]**. On the **First Specular Layer section**, set **Color** to **RGB [177, 75, 44]**.

On the **Second Specular Layer section**, set **Color** to **RGB [255, 123, 82]**. Take the render [see Figure E2].

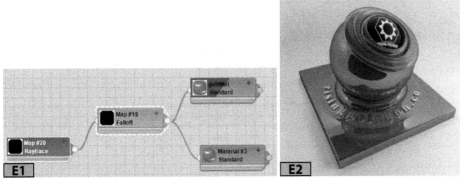

Exercise 3: Creating the Brass Material

In this exercise, we are going to create the brass material.

The following table summarizes the exercise.

Table E3: Creating the brass material	
Topics in this section:	• Getting Ready • Creating the Brass Material
Skill Level	Beginner
Project Folder	**unit-mt2**
Start File	**umt2-hoe2-end.max**
Final Exercise File	**umt2-hoe3-end.max**
Time to Complete	10 Minutes

Make sure the **umt2-hoe2-end.max** file that you created in Hands-on
Exercise 2 is open in 3ds Max.

Creating the Brass Material
Press M to open the **Slate Material Editor**, if not already open. Create
a copy of the **copperMat** node by **Shift** dragging it. Rename the node
as **brassMat** and then apply it to **geo1**, **geo2**, and **geo3**.

On the **Multi-Layer Basic Parameters** rollout, set **Diffuse** to **RGB [49,
38, 14]**. On the **First Specular Layer** section, set **Color** to **RGB [212,
154, 30]**. On the **Second Specular Layer** section, set **Color** to **RGB
[174, 98, 61]**. Take the render [see Figure E1] and then save the file
with the name **umt2-hoe3-end.max**.

Exercise 4: Creating the Chrome Material
In this exercise, we are going to create the chrome material.

The following table summarizes the exercise.

Table E4: Creating the chrome material	
Topics in this section:	• Getting Ready • Creating the Chrome Material
Skill Level	Beginner
Project Folder	**unit-mt2**
Start File	**umt2-hoe1-1to13-start.max**
Final Exercise File	**umt2-hoes4-end.max**
Time to Complete	10 Minutes

Getting Ready
Make sure the **hoes1-1to13-start.max** is open in 3ds Max.

Creating the Chrome Material
Load **umt2-hoe1-1to13-start.max** in 3ds Max. Press **M** to open the **Slate
Material Editor**. On the **Material/Map/Browser | Materials | General**
rollout, drag the **Standard** material to the active view. Rename the
material as **chromeMat**. Apply the material to **geo1**, **geo2**, and **geo3**.
Save the scene as **umt2-hoes4-end.max**.

On the **Parameter Editor | chromeMat | Blinn Basic Parameters** rollout,
click the **Diffuse** color swatch. On the **Color Selector : Diffuse Color**
dialog, set **Value** to **12** and click **OK**. On the **Specular Highlights**
section, set **Specular Level** to **150** and **Glossiness** to **80**.

On the **Maps** rollout, set **Reflection** to **90** and then click the **Reflection** map button. On the **Material Map Browser** that appears, double-click **Raytrace**. On the **Raytrace** map | **Raytracer Parameters** | **Background** section, click **None**. On the **Material/Map Browser** that appears, double-click **Bitmap**. In the **Select Bitmap Image File** dialog that appears, select **refMap.jpeg**. Render the scene [see Figure E1].

Exercise 5: Creating the Brushed Aluminum Material

In this exercise, we are going to create the brushed aluminum material using Photoshop and 3ds Max. The following table summarizes the exercise.

Table E5: Creating the brushed aluminum material	
Topics in this section:	• Getting Ready • Creating the Brushed Aluminum Material
Skill Level	Beginner
Project Folder	**unit-mt2**
Start File	**umt2-hoe1-1to13-start.max**
Final Exercise File	**umt2-hoe5-end.max**
Time to Complete	15 Minutes

Getting Ready

Make sure the **umt2-hoe1-1to13-start.max** is open in 3ds Max.

Creating the Brushed Aluminum Material

Start Photoshop. Create a **1000 x 1000 px** document and fill it with **50%** gray color. Choose **Noise | Add Noise** from the **Filter** menu and then set the parameters as shown in Figure E1 and then click **OK**. Choose **Blur | Motion Blur** from the **Filter** menu and then set the parameters as shown in Figure E2 and then click **OK**.

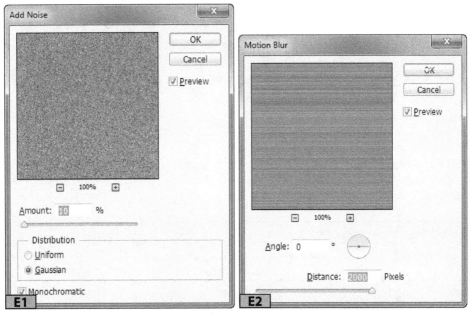

Choose **Adjustments | Brightness\Contrast** from the **Image** menu and then set the parameters as shown in Figure E3 and then click **OK**. Save the document as **scratch.jpg**.

Load **umt2-hoe1-1to13-start.max** in 3ds Max, if not already loaded. Press **M** to open the **Slate Material Editor**. On the **Material/Map Browser | Materials | General** rollout, drag the **Standard** material to the active view. Rename the material as **balMat**. Apply the material to **geo1**, **geo2**, and **geo3**.

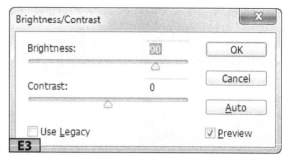

On the **Parameter Editor | balMat | Shader Basic Parameters** rollout, choose **Oren-Nayar-Blinn** from the drop-down. On the **Parameter Editor | balMat | Oren-Nayar-Blinn Basic Parameters** rollout, click **Ambient** color swatch. On the **Color Selector : Ambient Color** dialog, set **Value** to **84** and click **OK**. Unlock the **Ambient** and **Diffuse** components of the material.

Click the **Diffuse** map button and then on the **Material/Map Browser** that appears, double-click **Mix**. On the **Parameter Editor | Mix map**, set **Color 1** to **127** and assign **scratch.jpg** to **Color 2** using the **Bitmap** map. Set **Mix** Amount to **72%**. On the **balMat | Oren-Nayar-Blinn Basic Parameters** rollout | **Advanced Diffuse** section, set **Diffuse Level** to **81**, and **Roughness** to **80**. Now, take a test render [see Figure E4].

On the **Parameter Editor | balMat | Oren-Nayar-Blinn Basic Parameters** rollout | **Specular Highlight** section, set **Specular Level** to **156**, **Glossiness** to **13**, and **Soften** to **0.48**. Now, take a test render [see Figure E5]. On the **Parameter Editor | scratch.jpg | Output** rollout, set **Output Amount** to **0.6**. Take a render [see Figure E6]. Save the file as **umt2-hoe5-end.max**.

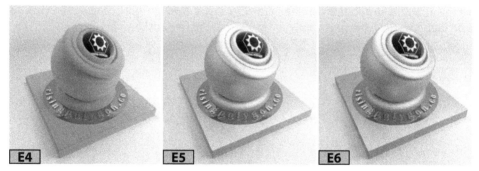

Exercise 6: Creating the Denim Fabric Material

In this exercise, we are going to create the denim fabric material using Photoshop and 3ds Max.

The following table summarizes the exercise.

Table E6: Creating the denim fabric material	
Topics in this section:	• Getting Ready • Creating the Denim Fabric Material
Skill Level	Beginner

Project Folder	**unit-mt2**
Start File	**umt2-hoe1-1to13-start.max**
Final Exercise File	**umt2-hoe6-end.max**
Time to Complete	15 Minutes

Getting Ready
Make sure the **umt2-hoe1-1to13-start.max** is open in 3ds Max.

Creating the Denim Fabric Material
Start Photoshop. Create a **1000 x 1000 px** document and fill it with **RGB [41, 67, 102]** color. Create a new layer and fill it with **50%** gray. Press **D** to switch to the default colors. Choose **Filter Gallery| Sketch | Halftone Pattern** from the **Filter** menu and then set the parameters as shown in Figure E1 and then click **OK**. Choose **Pixelate | Mezzotint** from the **Filter** menu and then set the parameters as shown in Figure E2 and then click **OK**.

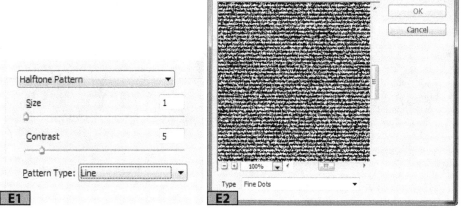

Duplicate the layer and rotate and scale the duplicate layer [see Figure E3]. Choose **Blur | Gaussian Blur** from the **Filter** menu and then apply a blur of radius **1**. Set blending mode to **Multiply**. Also, set the blending mode of the middle layer [Layer 1] to **Softlight** [Figure E4].

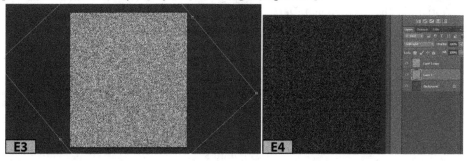

Save the file as **denimFebric.jpg**. Choose **Flatten Image** from the **Layer** menu to flatten the image. Now, press **Ctrl+Shift+U** to desaturate the image and then save it as **denimFebricBump.jpg**. In 3ds Max, press **M** to open the **Slate Material Editor**. On the **Material/Map Browser | Materials | Scanline** rollout, drag the **Standard** material to the active view. Rename the material as **denimMat**. Apply the material to **geo1**, **geo2**, and **geo3**.

Save the scene as **umt2-hoe6-end.max**. On the **Parameter Editor | denimMat | Shader Basic Parameters** rollout, choose **Oren-Nayar-Blinn** from the drop-down. On the **Parameter Editor | denimMat | Oren-Nayar-Blinn Basic Parameters** rollout, click **Ambient** color swatch.

On the **Color Selector : Ambient Color** dialog, set **RGB** to **50**, **53**, and **57** and click **OK**. Unlock the **Ambient** and **Diffuse** components of the material. Click the **Diffuse** map button and then on the **Material Map Browser** that appears, double-click **Bitmap**. Assign **denimFebric.jpg**. On the **denimMat | Oren-Nayar-Blinn Basic Parameters** rollout | **Advanced Diffuse** section, set **Diffuse Level** to **250**, and **Roughness** to **75**. Now, take a test render [see Figure E5].

On the **Parameter Editor | denimMat | Oren-Nayar-Blinn Basic Parameters** rollout | **Specular Highlight** section, set **Specular Level** to **7**, and **Glossiness** to **10**. Take a test render [see Figure E6]. On the **Maps** rollout, ensure **Bump** is set to **30%** and then click **Bump** map button.

On the **Material/Map Browser** that appears, double-click **Bitmap**. On the **Select Bitmap Image File** dialog that appears, select **denimFebricBump.jpg**. Take a test render [see Figure E7].

E5   E6   E7

Exercise 7: Creating the Blend Material

In this exercise, we are going to create a blend material.

The following table summarizes the exercise.

Table E7: Working with the blend material	
Topics in this section:	• Getting Ready • Working with the Blend Material
Skill Level	Beginner
Project Folder	**unit-mt2**
Start File	**umt2-hoe1-1to13-start.max**
Final Exercise File	**umt2-hoe7-end.max**
Time to Complete	15 Minutes

Getting Ready
Make sure the **umt2-hoe1-1to13-start.max** is open in 3ds Max.

Working with the Blend Material

Save the scene as **umt2-hoe7-end.max**. Press **M** to open the **Slate Material Editor**. On the **Material/Map Browser | Materials | General** rollout, drag the **Blend** material to the active view. Rename the materials connected to the **Blend** node as **mat1** and **mat2**. Apply the **Blend** material to **geo1**, **geo2**, and **geo3**.

Assign **ConcreteBare.jpg** to the **mat1 | Diffuse** map and **ConcreteBare1.jpg** to the **mat2 | Diffuse** map. Take a test render [see Figure E1]. Assign a **Noise** map to the **Blend** material's **Mask** control. On the **Mixing Curve** section, turn on the **Use Curve** switch and set **Upper** to **0.78** and **Lower** to **0.3**. Take a test render [see Figure E2].

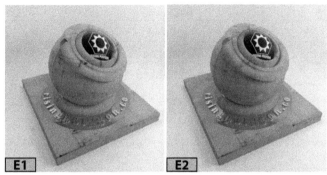

On the **Parameter Editor | Noise Parameters** rollout, set **Noise Type** to **Fractal**, **High** to **0.9**, and **Size** to **15.5**. Take a test render and press **Ctrl+S** to save the file. For the sake of clarity, I have rendered [see Figure E3] a plane with **mat1** (left image), **mat2** (middle image), and **Blend** (right image) materials applied. Figure E4 shows the node network.

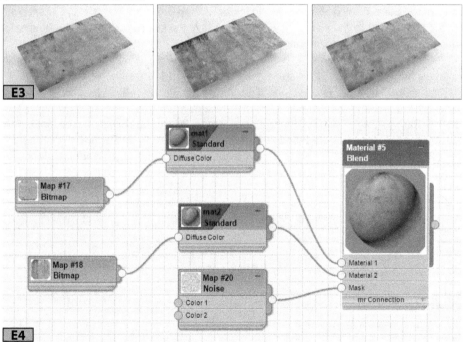

In this exercise, we are going to create a double-sided material.

The following table summarizes the exercise.

Table E8: Working with the double-sided material	
Topics in this section:	• Getting Ready • Working with the Double-Sided Material
Skill Level	Beginner
Project Folder	**unit-mt2**
Start File	**umt2-hoe1-1to13-start.max**
Final Exercise File	**umt2-hoe8-end.max**
Time to Complete	15 Minutes

Getting Ready

Make sure the **umt2-hoe1-1to13-start.max** is open in 3ds Max. Save file as **umt2-hoe8-end.max**.

Working with the Double Sided Material

Delete **geo4**, **geo1**, **geo6** from the scene and place a teapot at the center of **geo5**. Go to the **Modify** panel and then on the **Parameters** rollout | **Teapot Parts** section, turn off **Handle**, **Spout**, and **Lid** switches. Also, set **Segments** to **32**.

Press **M** to open the **Slate Material Editor**. On the **Material/Map Browser** | **Materials** | **General** rollout, drag the **Double Sided** material to the active view. Rename the materials connected to the **DoubleSided** node as **mat1** and **mat2**. Apply the material to the teapot.

Now, we will assign maps to the back and facing materials of the **Double Sided** material. The **Facing Material** is represented by **mat1** whereas the **Back Material** is represented by **mat2**.

Assign **ConcreteBare.jpg** to the **mat1** | **Diffuse** map. Assign a **Perlin Marble** map to the **mat2** | **Diffuse** map. Set **Translucency** to **25** in the **Double Sided** material | **Double Sided Basic Parameters** rollout. Take a test render [see Figure E1] and press **Ctrl+S** to save the file. Figure E2 shows the node network.

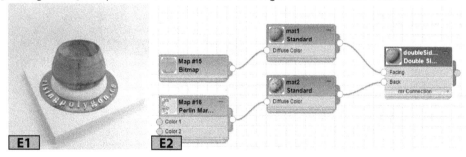

Exercise 9: Creating the Shellac Material

In this exercise, we are going to create a **Shellac** material.

The following table summarizes the exercise.

Table E9: Working with the **Shellac** material	
Topics in this section:	• Getting Ready • Working with the **Shellac** Material
Skill Level	Beginner
Project Folder	**unit-mt2**
Start File	**umt2-hoe8-end.max**
Final Exercise File	**umt2-hoe9-end.max**
Time to Complete	15 Minutes

Getting Ready

Make sure the **umt2-hoe8-end.max** is open in 3ds Max. Save it as **umt2-hoe9-end.max**. Turn on the **Lid** for the teapot.

Working with the Shellac Material

Press **M** to open the **Slate Material Editor**. On the **Material/Map Browser | Materials | General** rollout, drag the **Shellac** material to the active view.

Rename the materials connected to the **Base Material** and **Shellac Mat** ports of the **Shellac** node as **mat1** and **mat2**, respectively. Apply the material to the teapot.

Assign the **Swirl** map to the **mat1 | Diffuse** map and **Wood** map to the **mat2 | Diffuse** map. Set **Shellac Color Blend** to **86** in the **Shellac Basic Parameters** rollout. Take a test render [see Figure E1].

E1

Exercise 10: Creating the Microscopic Material

In this exercise, we're going to create a microscopic material [see Figure E1]. The following material(s) and map(s) are used in this exercise: **Standard**, **Mix**, **Falloff**, and **Noise**.

The following table summarizes the exercise.

Table E10: Creating the microscopic material	
Topics in this section:	• Getting Ready • Creating the Microscopic Material
Skill Level	Beginner
Project Folder	**unit-mt2**

Start File	umt2-hoe10-start.max
Final Exercise File	umt2-hoe10-end.max
Time to Complete	15 Minutes

Getting Ready
Make sure the **umt2-hoe10-start.max** is open in 3ds Max.

Creating the Microscopic Material
Press **M** to open the **Slate Material Editor** and then create a new **Standard** material and assign it to the **sphGeo** in the scene. Rename the material as **msMat**. Connect a **Falloff** map to the **msMat's Diffuse** port. On the **Parameter Editor | Falloff** map | **Falloff Parameters** rollout | **Front:Side** section, set first color swatch to **RGB [20, 20, 20]** and second color swatch to white. Set **Falloff Type** to **Perpendicular/Parallel**. Ensure **Falloff Direction** is set to **Viewing Direction (Camera Z-Axis)** [see Figure E2]. Also, set the **Mix Curve** to as shown in Figure E3.

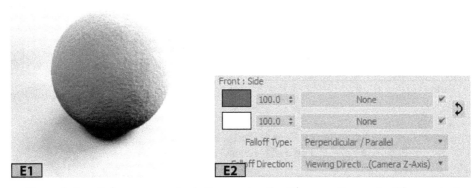

Now, you will create two **Noise** maps and mix them using the **Mix** map. Connect a **Mix** map to the **msMat's Bump** port. On the **Parameter Editor | Mix** map | **Mix Parameters** rollout, set **Mix Amount** to **37.8**. On the **Slate Material Editor**, connect two **Noise** maps, one each to the **Color 1** and **Color 2** ports. For the **Color 1 | Noise** map use the settings shown in Figure E4. Figure E5 shows the **Noise** map settings connected to **Color 2**. Figure E6 shows the node network.

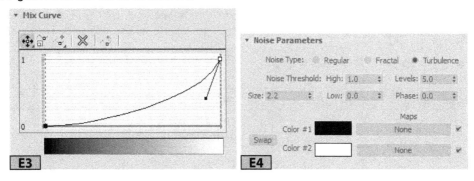

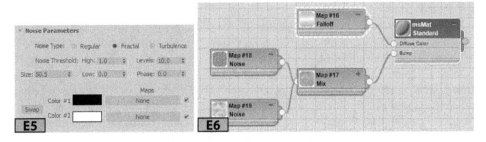

Now, render the scene. Notice that the output is little bit on the darker side. To address this, on the **Parameter Editor | Falloff** map | **Falloff Parameters** rollout | **Front:Side** section, set first color swatch to **RGB [80, 80, 80]**. Render the scene [see Figure E1].

Exercise 11: Creating Material for a Volleyball

Here, we are going to apply texture to a volleyball [see Figure E1]. Right image in Figure E1 shows the reference whereas the left image shows the rendered output. The following material(s) and map(s) are used in this exercise: **Multi/Sub-Object**, **Standard**, and **Noise**.

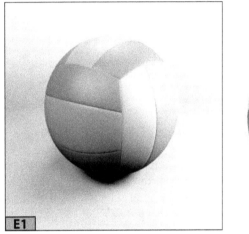

The following table summarizes the exercise.

Table E11: Creating material for a volleyball	
Topics in this section:	• Getting Ready • Creating Material for a Volleyball
Skill Level	Beginner
Project Folder	**unit-mt2**
Start File	**umt2-hoe11-start.max**
Final Exercise File	**umt2-hoe11-end.max**
Time to Complete	15 Minutes

Getting Ready

Make sure the **umt2-hoe11-start.max** is open in 3ds Max. Save the file as **umt2-hoe11-end.max**.

Creating Material for a Volleyball

Select the **VolleyBallGeo** in any viewport and then go to the **Modify** panel. On the **Selection** rollout, click **Element** and then select the elements that make the yellow part of the volleyball [see Figure E2]. See the right image in Figure E1 for reference.

On the **Modify panel | Polygon: Material IDs** rollout, set **ID** to **1** [see Figure E3]. Similarly, select the blue and white elements and assign them ID **2** and **3**, respectively. Press **M** to open the **Slate Material Editor** and then create a new **Multi/Sub-object** material and assign it to the **VolleyBallGeo** in the scene. Rename the material as **vbMat**. On the **Parameter Editor | vbMat | Multi/Sub-Object Parameters** rollout, click **Set Number** and then set **Number of Materials** to **3** in the dialog that appears. Next, click **OK**. In the **Slate Material Editor**, connect a **Standard** material to the port **1** of the **vbMat**. On the **Parameter Editor | Blinn Basic Parameter** rollout, set the **Diffuse** component to **RGB [242, 140, 8]**. On the **Specular Highlights** section, set **Specular Level** to **71** and **Glossiness** to **28**.

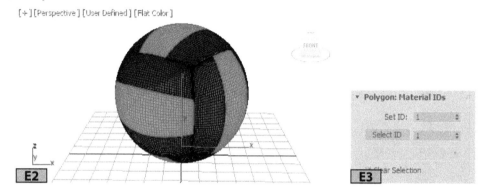

Connect a **Noise** map to the **Bump** port of the **Standard** material. Set **Bump** to **2%**. On the **Parameter Editor | Noise map | Noise Parameters** rollout, set **Noise Type** to **Turbulence**, **Levels** to **9**, and **Size** to **0.5**. On the **Slate Material Editor**, select the **Standard** material and **Noise** map. Now, create a copy of the selected nodes using **SHIFT**. Connect the new Standard material to the port **2** of the **vbMat**. Similarly, create another copy and connect it to port **3**. Figure E4 shows the node network. Set **Diffuse** components of the material connected to the port **2** and **3** to **RGB [11, 91, 229]** and **RGB [236, 236, 230]**, respectively. Now, press F9 to take a render.

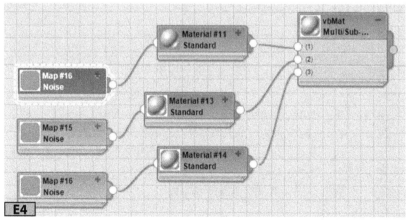

Exercise 12: Creating Material for a Water Tunnel

Here, we are going to apply texture to a water tunnel [see Figure E1]. The following material(s) and map(s) are used in this exercise: **Raytrace**, **Standard**, **Mix**, and **Noise**.

E1

The following table summarizes the exercise.

Table E12: Creating material for a water tunnel	
Topics in this section:	• Getting Ready • Creating Material for a Water Tunnel
Skill Level	Beginner
Project Folder	**unit-mt2**
Start File	**umt2-hoes12-start.max**
Final Exercise File	**umt2-hoes12-end.max**
Time to Complete	15 Minutes

Getting Ready

Make sure the **umt2-hoes12-start.max** is open in 3ds Max.

Creating Material for a Water Tunnel

Press **M** to open the **Slate Material Editor** and then create a new **Raytrace** material and assign it to the **waterGeo** in the scene. Rename the material as **waterMat**. On the **Parameter Editor | Raytrace Basic Parameter** rollout, set **Diffuse** to black. Set **Transparency** to **RGB (146, 175, 223)**. Set **Reflect** to **RGB [178, 178, 178]**. On the **Specular Highlight** section, set **Specular Level** to **161** and **Glossiness** to **29**. Connect a **Noise** map to the **Bump** port of the **waterMat**. Use the default values for the **Noise** map. Press **F9** to render the scene [Figure E2].

On the **Slate Material Editor**, create a new **Standard** material and assign it to the **caveGeo** in the scene. Rename the material as **caveMat**. Connect a **Mix** map to the **Diffuse** port of the **caveMat**. Connect a **Noise** map to the **Color 1** port of the **Mix** map. On the **Noise Parameters** rollout, set **Noise Type** to **Turbulence**, **Levels** to **10**, **Size** to **31.7**. Set **Color 1** to **RGB [132, 77, 6]** and **Color 2** to **RGB [154, 100, 79]**. Connect a **Noise** map to the **Color 2** port of the **Mix** map. On the **Noise Parameters** rollout, set **Noise Type** to **Turbulence**, **Levels** to **10**, **Size** to **72**. Set **Color 1** to **RGB [212, 84, 45]** and **Color 2** to **RGB [181, 99, 54]**.

On the **Parameter Editor | Mix Parameters** rollout, set **Mix Amount** to **40**. On the **Mixing curve** section, turn on the **Use Curve** switch and then set **Upper** to **0.6** and **Lower** to **0.53**. Take a test render [Figure E3].

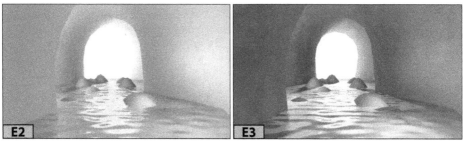

Connect a **Mix** map to the **Displacement** port of the **caveMat**. Set **Displacement** to **25%**. Connect a **Noise** map to the **Color 1** port of the **Mix** map. On the **Noise Parameters** rollout, set **Noise Type** to **Turbulence**, **Levels** to **8.4**, **Size** to **21.2**. Connect a **Noise** map to the **Color 2** port of the **Mix** map. On the **Noise Parameters** rollout, set **Noise Type** to **Turbulence**, **Levels** to **10**, **Size** to **81.5**. On the **Parameter Editor | Mix Parameters** rollout, set **Mix Amount** to **18.4**. Take a test render [Figure E4].

Similarly, create a material for the **floorGeo**. If you want to see the values I have used, open **umt2-hoe12-end.max** and check the **floorMat** material.

Exercise 13: Creating Rusted Metal Texture

Let's now create a rusted metal texture [see Figure E1]. The following material(s) and map(s) are used in this exercise: **Standard, Composite, Bitmap, Color Correction**, and **Noise**. The following table summarizes the exercise.

Table E13: Creating rusted metal texture	
Topics in this section:	• Getting Ready • Creating Rusted Metal Texture
Skill Level	Beginner
Project Folder	**unit-mt2**
Start File	**umt2-hoe1-1to13-start.max**
Final Exercise File	**umt2-hoe13-end.max**
Time to Complete	15 Minutes

Getting Ready

Make sure the **umt2-hoe1-1to13-start.max** is open in 3ds Max. Save the file with the name **umt2-hoe13-end.max**.

Creating Rusted Metal Texture

Press **M** to open the **Slate Material Editor**. In the **Material/Map Browser | Materials | General** rollout, double-click on **Standard** to add a **Standard** material to the active view. Rename the material as **rustMat** and apply it to **geo1**, **geo2**, and **geo3**.

In the **Parameter Editor | Shader Basic Parameters** rollout, turn on the **2-Sided** switch. Connect a **Composite** map to the **rustMap's Diffuse Color** port. Now, connect **rust.jpg** to the **Composite** map's **Layer 1** port [see Figure E2].

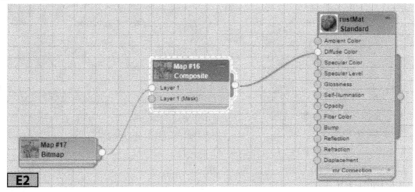

On the **Parameter Editor | Composite** map **| Composite Layers | Layer 1** rollout, click **Add a New Layer** button to add a new layer [see Figure E3]. Notice that a new port with the name **Layer 2** has been added to the **Composite** map node in the active view. Connect **rustPaint.jpg** to the **Composite** map's **Layer 2** port. On the **Parameter Editor | Composite** map **| Composite Layers | Layer 2** rollout, set **Opacity** to **10%** and blend mode to **Color Dodge** [see Figure E4].

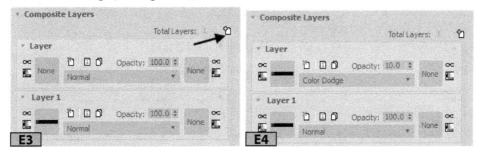

Now, take a test render [see Figure E5]. Connect **scratchesMask.jpg** to the **Composite** map's **Layer 2 (Mask)** port using a **Bitmap** map. Now, check the **Invert** checkbox from the **Bitmap's Output** rollout. Take a test render [see Figure E6]. On the **Slate Material Editor's** active view, create copy of the **Bitmap** node connected to the **Composite** map's **Layer 2 (Mask)** node using **Shift**. Connect the duplicate node to the **Bump** node of **rustMat**. On the **Parameter Editor | rustMat | Maps** rollout, set bump map's strength to **10%** and then take a test render [see Figure E7].

In this exercise, we are going to apply materials and textures to an outdoor scene [see Figure E1]. The following table summarizes the exercise.

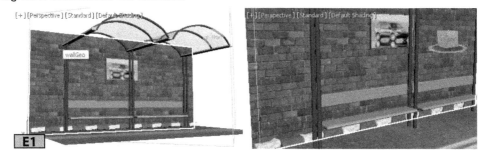

Table E14: Shading an outdoor scene	
In this exercise, you will:	• Apply material to the objects • Use the **UVW Map** modifier • Apply textures to the material
Topics in this section:	• Getting Ready • Shading the Scene
Skill Level	Intermediate
Project Folder	**unit-mt2**
Start File	**umt2-hoe14-start.max**
Final Exercise File	**umt2-hoe14-end.max**
Time to Complete	30 Minutes

Getting Ready

Make sure the **umt2-hoe14-start.max** is open in 3ds Max. Save the file with the name **umt2-hoe14-end.max**.

Shading the Scene

Select **wallGeo** from the **Scene Explorer** and then press **M** to open the **Slate Material Editor**. Drag **Standard** from the **Material/Map Browser | Maps | Scanline** rollout to the **Active View**. Rename the material as **wallMat**. RMB click on the **wallMat** node and then choose **Assign Material to Selection**. Again, RMB click and then choose **Show Shaded Material in Viewport**.

In the **Active View**, drag the **Diffuse Color** socket onto the empty area and release the mouse button. Choose **General | Bitmap** from the popup menu. In the **Select Bitmap Image File** dialog that opens, select **redBrick.png** and then click **Open** to make a connection between the **Diffuse Color** socket and texture. Double-click on the **Bitmap** node and then in the **Parameter Editor | Coordinates** rollout, set **U Tiling** and **V Tiling** to **4**. Similarly, connect the **Bump** socket to the **redBrickGray.png** and set **Tiling** to **4**.

Notice in the viewport the map is displayed on the wall [see the left image in Figure E2]. Ensure **wallGeo** is selected in the **Scene Explorer** and then go to **Modify** panel and add the **UVW Map** modifier to the stack. Select the modifier's **Gizmo** and scale the texture so that the size of the bricks appear in right proportions [see the right image in Figure E2].

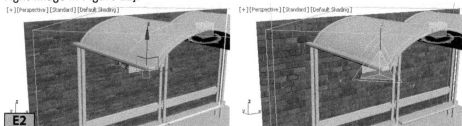

Select **floorGeo** from the **Scene Explorer** and then in the **Slate Material Editor**, drag **Standard** from the **Material/Map Browser | Maps | General** rollout to the **Active View**. Rename the material as **roadMat**. RMB click on the **roadMat** node and then choose **Assign Material to Selection**. Again, RMB click and then choose **Show Shaded Material in Viewport**. In the **Active View**, drag the **Diffuse Color** socket onto the empty area and release the mouse button. Choose **General | Bitmap** from the popup menu. In the **Select Bitmap Image File** dialog that opens, select **road.jpg** and then click **Open** to make a connection between the **Diffuse Color** socket and texture. Notice in the viewport, the texture appears on the **floorGeo** [see Figure E3]. Now, we need to change the direction of the yellow line. We will do so by using the **UVW Map** modifier.

Ensure **floorGeo** is selected in the **Scene Explorer** and then go to **Modify** panel and add the **UVW Map** modifier to the stack. Select the modifier's **Gizmo** and rotate it by **90** degrees by using the **Rotate** tool. You can also use the **Move** tool to position the texture on the geometry [see Figure E4].

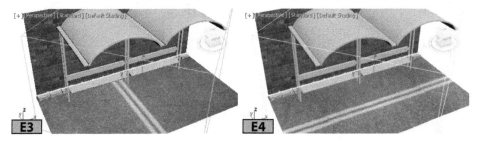

Now, we will apply the material to billboard. We will use the **Multi/Subobject** material. The ID **1** has been assigned to the screen component of the board whereas rest of the geometry is held by ID **2**. Select **billBoardGeo** from the **Scene Explorer** and then add a **Multi/Subobject** node to the **Active View**. Rename the material as **billboardMat**. In the **Parameter Editor**, click **Set Number**. Now, in the **Set Number of Materials** dialog, set **Number of Materials** field to **2** and click **OK**. RMB click on the **billboardMat** node and then choose **Assign Material to Selection**.

Drag the **1** socket to the empty area of the view and then choose **Materials | Scanline | Standard** from the popup menu. Connect the **Standard's** materials **Diffuse Color** socket to the **honda.jpg**. Connect another **Standard** material to the **2** socket of the **billboardMat**. In the **Parameter Editor | Blinn Basic Parameters rollout | Specular Highlight** group of the **Standard** material, set **Specular Level** and **Glossiness** to **92** and **33**, respectively. Also, set **Diffuse** color to **RGB [20, 20, and 20]**. The material appears on the **billBoardGeo** in the viewport [see Figure E5]. You need to enable **Show Shaded Material in Viewport** for the two Standard materials. Create two **Standard** materials and assign dark gray and yellow colors to them. Now, apply these materials to alternate brick from the **brickGrp** group [see Figure E6].

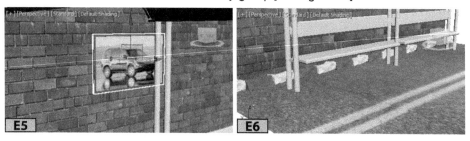

Now, create a chrome material as done in Exercise 4. Do not assign the **refMap.jpg** to the **Raytrace** map. In the **Scene Explorer**, select **bsGeo11, bsGeo12, bsGeo15, bsGeo16, bsGeo18, bsGeo19, bsGeo20, bsGeo22, bsGeo23, bsGeo24, bsGeo26,** and **bsGeo27**. Assign chrome material to the selected objects [see Figure E7]. Also, assign chrome material to **bsGeo3,** and **bsGeo6**.

In the **Scene Explorer**, select **bsGeo04, bsGeo05, bsGeo07,** and **bsGeo08**. Drag **Standard** from the **Material/Map Browser | Maps | General** rollout to the **Active View**. Rename the material as **woodMat**. RMB click on the **woodMat** node and then choose **Assign Material to Selection**. Again, RMB click and then choose **Show Shaded Material in Viewport**. In the **Active View**, drag the **Diffuse Color** socket onto the empty area and release the mouse button. Choose **General | Wood** from the popup menu. In the **Parameter Editor | Wood | Wood Parameters** rollout, change **Color #2** to **RGB[106, 25, 0]**. The wood texture is displayed in the viewport [see Figure E8].

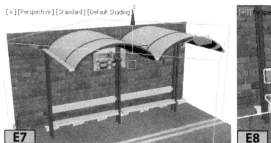

In the **Scene Explorer**, select **bsGeo21,** and **bsGeo25** and then drag **Standard** from the **Material/Map Browser | Maps | General** rollout to the **Active View**. Rename the material as **roofMat**. RMB click on the **roofMat** node and then choose **Assign Material to Selection**. Again, RMB click and then choose **Show Shaded Material in Viewport**. In the **Parameter Editor | roofMat | Blinn Basic Parameters** rollout, change **Diffuse** to **RGB[23, 241, 12]** and then set **Opacity** to **25**. Figure E9 shows the roof material in the viewport.

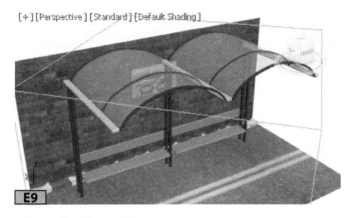

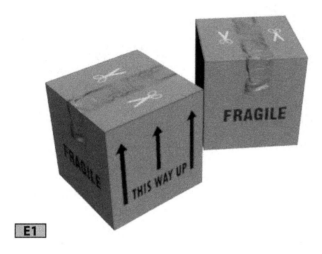

Exercise 15: Texturing a Cardboard Box

Let's start by texturing a cardboard box [see Figure E1] using the **UV Editor**.

The following Table summarizes the exercise.

Table E15: Texturing a cardboard texture	
Topics in this section:	• Getting Ready • Texturing the Cardboard Box
Skill Level	Intermediate
Project Folder	**unit-mt2**
Final Exercise File	**umt2-hoe15-end.max**
Time to Complete	20 Minutes

Getting Ready

Reset 3ds Max. Set units to **Generic Units** and then create a box with the **Length**, **Height**, and **Width** set to **190**.

Texturing the Cardboard Box

Ensure the box is selected in a viewport and then go to **Modify** panel. Add the **Unwrap UVW** modifier to the stack. Click **Polygon** 🔲 on the **Selection** panel and then press **Ctrl+A** to select all polygons. On the **Projection** rollout, click **Box Map** 🔲 and then click again to deactivate. On the **Edit UVs** rollout, click **Open UV Editor** to open the **Edit UVWs** window. Choose **Unfold Mapping** from the **Mapping** menu of the window. The **Unfold Mapping** dialog appears. Click **OK** to accept the default settings and unfold UVs [see Figure E2].

Choose **Pick Texture** from the drop-down located on the top-right corner of the window, the **Material/Map Browser** appears. In the browser, double-click on **Bitmap** from the **Maps | General** rollout. In the **Select Bitmap Image File** dialog, select **cardboard_texture.png** and click **Open**. The **cardboard_texture.png** appears in the **Edit UVWs** window [see Figure E3].

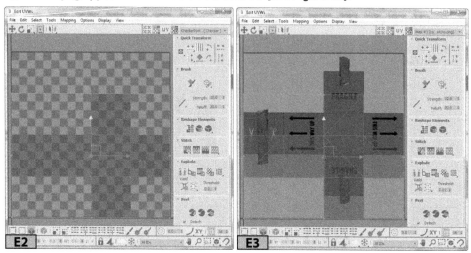

Click **Vertex** from the bottom-left corner of the window to activate the **Vertex** selection mode. All the vertices are selected. If they are not selected, press **Ctrl+A** to select them. Ensure **Move Selected Subobjects** ✛ is active from the window's toolbar and then align all UVs to the background texture [see Figure E4]. Press and hold **Shift** while dragging to constrain the movement.

Now, select a complete column of row of the vertices and align them with the background texture [see Figure E5]. You can also select vertices in a viewport. If the UVs are not in the straight line, you can use **Align Horizontally to Pivot** and **Align Vertically to Pivot** from the **Quick Transform** rollout of the window to straighten the UVs. Close the Edit UVWs window.

Press **M** to open the **Slate Material Editor**. From the **Material/Map Browser | Material** rollout | **Scanline** rollout, double-click **Standard** to add it to the **Active View** and then assign it to the box in the scene. Rename the material as **boxMat**. Connect **ardboard_texture.png** texture to the **Diffuse** slot of the material. RMB click on **boxMat** node and choose **Show Shaded Material in Viewport** from the menu to display the texture in the viewport.

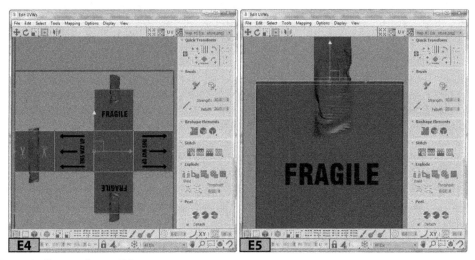

Exercise 16: Texturing a Dice

Let's start by texturing a dice [see Figure E1] using the **UV Editor**. In this Exercise we will export the UVs template to the Photoshop and then use Photoshop to create the texture. We will then import the texture back into 3ds Max and will apply it to the dice geometry.

E1

The following Table summarizes the exercise.

Table E16: Texturing a dice	
Topics in this section:	Getting Ready Texturing a Dice
Skill Level	Intermediate
Project Folder	**unit-mt2**
Final Exercise File	**umt2-hoe16-end.max**
Time to Complete	20 Minutes

Getting Ready

Reset 3ds Max. Set units to **Generic Units** and then create a box with the **Length**, **Height**, and **Width** set to **190**.

Texturing the Dice

Ensure the box is selected in a viewport and then go to **Modify** panel. Add the **Unwrap UVW** modifier to the stack. Click **Polygon** 🔲 on the **Selection** panel and then press **Ctrl+A** to select all polygons. On the **Projection** rollout, click **Box Map** 🔵 and then click again to deactivate.

On the **Edit UVs** rollout, click **Open UV Editor** to open the **Edit UVWs** window. Choose **Unfold Mapping** from the **Mapping** menu of the window. The **Unfold Mapping** dialog appears. Click **OK** to accept the default settings and unfold UVs. Choose **Render UV Template** from the **Tools** menu to open the **Render UVs** dialog. Click **Render UV Template** on the dialog. The **Render Map** window appears. Click **Save Image** on the window's toolbar to open the **Save Image** dialog. Type **dice_template** in the **File name** field and choose **PNG Image File** from the **Save as** type drop-down.

Click **Save** to save the template. Click **OK** from the **PNG Configuration** dialog. Now, close all windows and dialogs, if open. Open **dice_template.png** in **Photoshop**. **Layer 0** appears in the **Layers** panel. Create a new layer below **Layer 0** and fill it with **black** [see Figure E2].

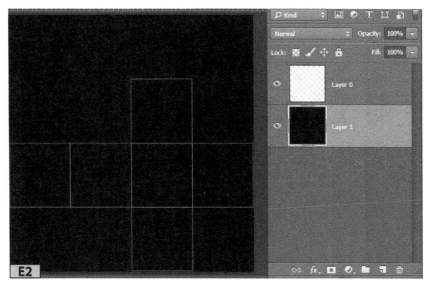

Now, using **Photoshop** tools and features create dice texture according to the dice template. I am putting simple numbers to identify the faces of the dice [see Figure E3]. You should go ahead and create a nice looking dice texture for your dice model.

Now, switch off the **black** layer and the **template** layer. Save the **Photoshop** document as **dice_texture.png**.

In 3ds Max, apply a **Standard** material to the box. Set **Diffuse color** to **red**. Connect **dice_texture.png** to the **Diffuse Color** and **Opacity** slots of the material's node, respectively. In the **dice_texture.png** map | **Bitmap Parameters** rollout, turn off the **Premultiplied Alpha** switch. Render the scene.

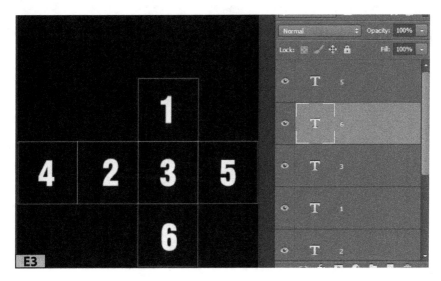

Exercise 17: Texturing a Dice - II

In this Exercise, we will use an alternate method to texture a dice. You will use six different maps for the six faces of the dice.

The following Table summarizes the exercise.

Table E17: Texturing a dice - II	
Topics in this section:	• Getting Ready • Texturing a Dice
Skill Level	Intermediate
Project Folder	**unit-mt2**
Final Exercise File	**umt2-hoe17-end.max**
Time to Complete	20 Minutes

Getting Ready

Reset 3ds Max. Set units to **Generic Units** and then create a box with the **Length**, **Height**, and **Width** set to **90**.

Texturing the Dice

Ensure the box is selected in a viewport and add the **UVW Map** modifier to the stack. Select **Box** in the **Mapping** group of the **Parameters** rollout. Click **Fit** on the **Alignment** group. RMB click on the box in a viewport and then choose **Convert To : Convert to Editable Poly** from the **Quad** menu.

Press **M** to open the **Slate Material Editor** and then from the **Material/Map Browser | General | Maps** rollout, drag **Standard** to the active view. Connect **side-1.jpg** to the **Diffuse** slot of the material. Similarly, add **5** more **Standard** maps and assign **side-2.jpg** to **side-6.jpg** to them. RMB click on the **Standard** material nodes and then choose **Show Shaded Material in Viewport** from the menu.

Now, add **a Multi/Sub-Object** node to the active view. In the **Parameter Editor**, click **Set Number**. Set **Number of Materials** to **6** and then click **OK**. Connect all **Standard** materials to the **Muli/Sub-Object** material. Figure E2 shows the node network. Figure E3 shows the maps in the viewport.

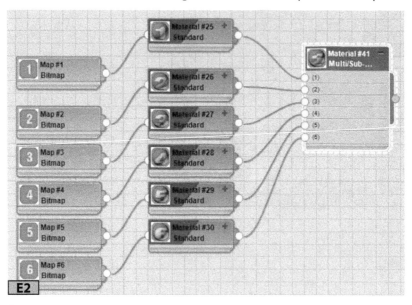

E2

Apply the **Muli/Sub-Object** material to the box in the scene. 3ds Max assigns the maps to the faces of the box. Now, if you want to change a map for a polygon, select that polygon in a viewport and then change the **ID** of the polygon from the **Polygon: Material IDs** rollout of the **Modify** panel.

You can use the **UV Editor** to change the orientation of the map. For example, if you want to change the orientation of the top face [see Figure E4], add **Unwrap UVW** modifier to the stack and then click **Polygon** from the **Selection** rollout. Select the top polygon and click **Open UV Editor** from the **Edit UVs** rollout. Press **A** to enable angel snap and then click **Rotate Selected Subobjects** from the toolbar. Now, rotate the selected polygon by **90** degrees to change the orientation of the map.

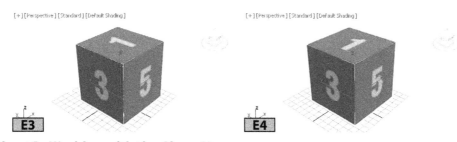

E3   E4

Exercise 18: Working with the ShapeMap

In this exercise, we will create a resolution independent map using the **ShapeMap**.

The following Table summarizes the exercise.

Table E18: Working with the ShapeMap	
Topics in this section:	• Getting Ready • Working with ShapeMap
Skill Level	Beginner
Project Folder	**unit-mt2**
Final Exercise File	**umt2-hoe18-end.max**
Time to Complete	20 Minutes

Getting Ready

Open **umt2-hoe18-start.max** in 3ds Max.

Working with the ShapeMap

Press **M** to open the **Slate Material Editor** and then from the **Material/Map Browser** | **General** | **Maps** rollout, drag **Standard** to the active view. Connect **ShapeMap** to the **Diffuse** slot of the material. Select the plane in the viewport. RMB click on the material node and then choose **Assign Material to Selection**.

Again, RMB click and then choose **Show Shaded Material in Viewport**. Notice only standard logo is displayed in the viewport at this moment [see Figure E1].

On the **Parameter Editor** | **ShapeMap** | **Shape Parameters** rollout, click **None** and then click the apple logo spline in any viewport. The shape is now displayed on the plane in the viewport [see Figure E2]. On the **Closed Shapes** section, turn on the **Render Outline** switch. On the **Outlines** section, set **Width** to **5**.

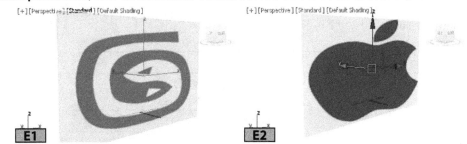

Set **Fill Color, Line Color, Background Color** to **RGB [141, 141, 141]**, **RGB [252, 255, 0]**, and **RGB [156, 188, 247]**, respectively. On the **Map Boundary** section, select **Manual** and then set **Width** and **Height** to **537**, and **300**, respectively.

The logo is now centered on the plane [see Figure E3]. Take a render [see Figure E4]. Now, if zoom in on an area of the logo and then render, you would notice that you will still get a high resolution output [see Figure E5].

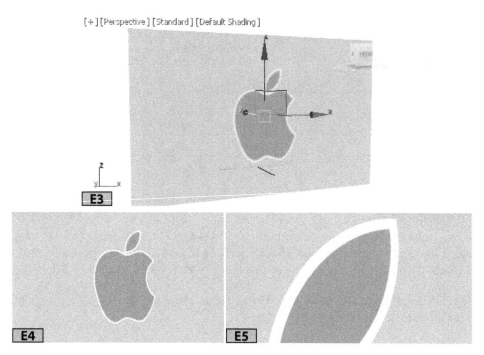

E3

E4

E5

Exercise 19: Working with Text Map

In this exercise, we will create a resolution independent map using the **Text Map**.

The following Table summarizes the exercise.

Table E19: Working with Text Map	
Topics in this section:	• Getting Ready • Working with Text Map
Skill Level	Beginner
Project Folder	**unit-mt2**
Final Exercise File	**umt2-hoe19-end.max**
Time to Complete	20 Minutes

Getting Ready

Open **umt2-hoe19-start.max** in 3ds Max.

Working with the Text Map

Press **M** to open the **Slate Material Editor** and then from the **Material/Map Browser | General | Maps** rollout, drag **Standard** to the active view. Connect **Text Map** to the **Diffuse** slot of the material. Select the plane in the viewport. RMB click on the material node and then choose **Assign Material to Selection**.

Again, RMB click and then choose **Show Shaded Material in Viewport**. Notice only standard logo is displayed in the viewport at this moment [see Figure E1].

On the **Parameter Editor | Text Map | Text Parameters** rollout, click **None** and then click the **TextPlus** object in any viewport. The text is now displayed on the plane in the viewport [see Figure E2]. On the **Characters** section, turn on the **Render Outline** switch. On the **Outlines** section, set **Width** to **5**.

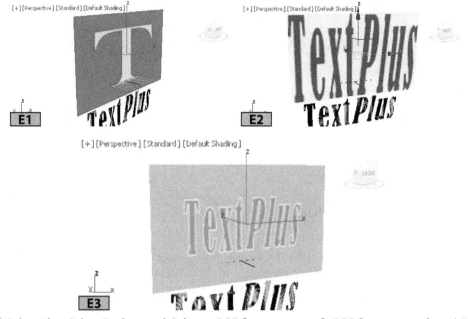

Set **Fill Color**, **Line Color**, **Background Color** to **RGB [141, 141, 141]**, **RGB [252, 255, 0]**, and **RGB [156, 188, 247]**, respectively. On the **Map Boundary** section, select **Manual** and then set **Width** and **Height** to **500**, and **200**, respectively.

The text is now centered on the plane [see Figure E3]. Take a render [see Figure E4]. Now, if zoom in on an area of the text and then render, you would notice that you will still get a high resolution output [see Figure E5].

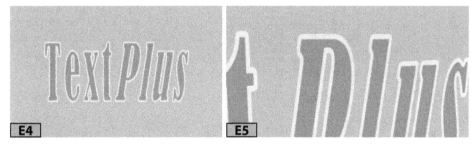

In this exercise, we will create a resolution independent map using the **TextureObjMask** map.

The following Table summarizes the exercise.

Table E20: Working with TextureObjMask map	
Topics in this section:	• Getting Ready • Working with TextureObjMask Map
Skill Level	Beginner
Project Folder	**unit-mt2**
Final Exercise File	**umt2-hoe20-end.max**
Time to Complete	20 Minutes

Getting Ready
Open **umt2-hoe20-start.max** in 3ds Max.

Working with the TextureObjMask Map
Press **M** to open the **Slate Material Editor** and then drag **TextureObjMask** to the active view. On the **Parameter Editor | TextureObjMask | Parameters** rollout, click **Control Object's None** button and then click on the sphere in a viewport to make it the control object.

Now, drag the **Cellular** and **Noise** maps to the active view. Change the color as desired and then connect Cellular map to the **Texture1** [outside texture] port of the **TextureObjMask** and **Noise** map to the **Texture2** [inside texture] port [see Figure E1]. In the **Parameter Editor | TextureObjMask | Parameters** rollout, set **Transition Range** to **25**.

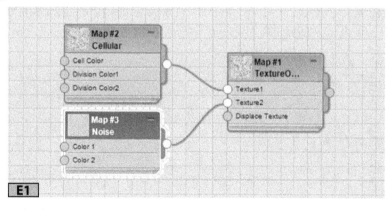

E1

Now, create a **Standard** material and connect its **Diffuse** port to the **TextureObjMask.** Select the plane in a viewport and RMB click on the material node and then choose **Assign Material to Selection**. Again, RMB click and then choose **Show Shaded Material in Viewport**. Take a test render [see Figure E2]. The sphere is obscuring the plane rendering. Create another **Standard** material and set its **Opacity** to **35**. Take a test render [see Figure E3].

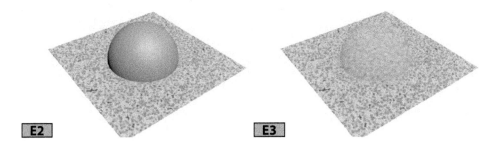

E2   E3

Summary
The unit covered the following topics:

- General/Scanline materials
- General maps

This page is intentionally left blank

Unit MT3-Physical, mental ray, and Autodesk Materials

3ds Max offers several materials that are used with the **mental ray** renderer. These materials are only visible in the **Material/Map Browser** if the active renderer is **NVIDIA mental ray** or **Quicksilver Hardware** renderer. The mental ray materials can be divided into three categories: Autodesk Materials, **Arch & Design** Material, and special-purpose mental ray materials.

In this unit, I'll describe the following:

- Autodesk Materials
- Arch & Design Material
- Physical Material

The **Physical** material is physically-based material and it is compatible with both the **ART** and **mental ray** renderers. Autodesk Materials are used to model commonly used surfaces in the construction, design, and the environment. These materials correspond to the materials found in other Autodesk products such as **Autodesk AutoCAD**, **Revit** and **Autodesk Inventor**. So, if you work between these applications, you can share surface and material information among them.

The mental ray **Arch & Design** material allows you improve rendering quality of the architectural renderings. This material is particularly useful when used to simulate glossy surfaces. The special-purpose mental ray materials are used to design special purpose materials such as car paint material, subsurface scattering material, and so forth.

Autodesk Materials

Autodesk Materials are based on the **Arch & Design** material. These materials work best when you use them with physically accurate lights such as photometric lights in a scene, modeled in the real-world units. However, the interface of the Autodesk materials is much simpler than the **Arch & Design** material, therefore, you can achieve good results in less time using Autodesk materials.

Many of the Autodesk materials use **Autodesk Bitmaps**. The **Autodesk Bitmap** is a simple bitmap type. This bitmap type always uses the real-world mapping coordinates. Therefore, if you have applied a **UVW Map** modifier to any geometry, make sure you turn on **Real-World Map Size** on the **Parameters** rollout. You can also change the default bitmap assignment.

Caution: Autodesk Bitmap compatibility
*3ds Max allows you to disconnect a bitmap, or replace it with another map. However, if you disconnect an **Autodesk Bitmap** in other application such as **Autodesk AutoCAD**, you won't be able to read the Autodesk material. If you are using other applications, make sure that you do not replace the bitmap with a map that only 3ds Max understands.*

Autodesk Ceramic

You can use this material to model the glazed ceramic material including porcelain.

Open **autoMat_begin.max**. Open the **Slate Material Editor**. On M**aterial/Map Browser** | **Materials** | **Autodesk**, double-click on **Autodesk Ceramic** to display the material's interface in the active view [see Figure F1]. Double-click on the material's node in the active view. In the **Material Editor** | **Ceramic** rollout, ensure that **Ceramic** is selected as **Type**. The **Ceramic** type produces look of earthenware.

Apply the material to teapot in the scene and take a test render [see Figure F2]. On the **Ceramic** rollout, set **Type** to **Porcelain**. Click **Color** swatch and change color to blue.

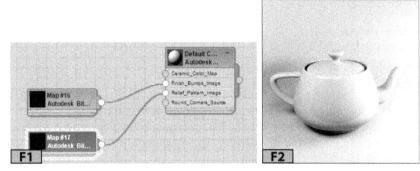

Color sets the color of the material. The other two options available for the **Color** control are **Use Map** and **Color By Object**. The **Use Map** option allows you to assign a map to color component of the material. If you set **Color** to **Color By Object**, 3ds Max uses the object's wireframe color as the material color. The **Finish** control lets you adjust the finish and reflectivity of the material.

Note: Color by object
*When you use the **Color By Object** option, the color appears on rendering but not in the viewport or material previews.*

Make sure **Finish** is set to **High Gloss / Glazed** and take a test render [see Figure 3]. Make sure **Finish** is set to **Satin** and take a test render [see Figure F4]. Make sure **Finish** is set to **Matte** and take a test render [see Figure F5]. Now, set **Finish** to **High Gloss / Glazed**.

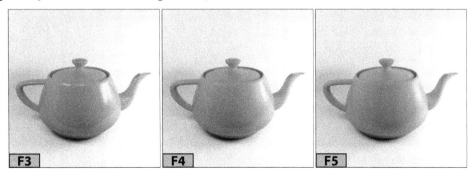

On the **Finish Bumps** rollout, check **Enable** and make sure **Type** is set to **Wavy** and **Amount** to **0.3**. Now, take a test render [see Figure F6].

The options in the **Finish Bumps** rollout can be used to simulate the patterns that appear in glaze during firing. You can also create custom bumps by using the **Custom** option from the **Type** drop-down. **Amount** sets the strength of the pattern to apply.

On the **Finish Bumps** rollout, turn off **Enable**. On the **Relief Pattern** rollout, turn on **Enable**. Click the **Image** button. On the **Parameters** rollout, click **Source None** button. Select **patten.jpg** from the **Select Bitmap Image File** dialog and click **Open**. On the **Relief Pattern** rollout, set **Amount** to **1.2** and take a test render [see Figure F7].

F6   F7

The options in the **Relief Pattern** rollout allow you to model a pattern stamped into the clay. **Amount** controls the height of the relief pattern.

Autodesk Concrete

This material allows you to model the concrete material. Figure F8 shows its interface. The **Sealant** control of the **Concrete** rollout, controls the reflectiveness of the surface. **None** [see Figure F9] does not affect the surface finish. **Epoxy** [see Figure F10] adds a reflective coating on the surface whereas **Acrylic** [see Figure F11] adds a matte reflective coating.

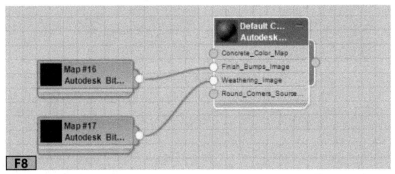

F8

The **Type** control in the **Finish Bumps** area allows you to set the texture of the concrete. **Broom Straight** which is a default type, specifies a straight broom pattern [see Figure F12]. **Broom Curved** uses a curving broom pattern [see Figure F13]. **Smooth** creates a pattern with speckled irregularities [see Figure F14].

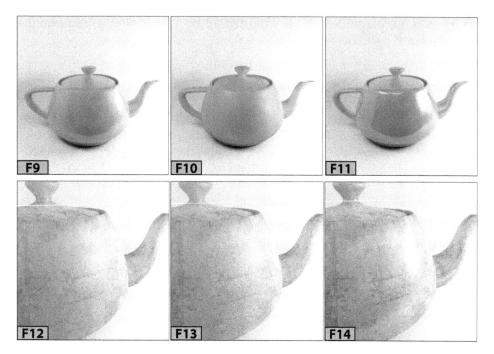

Polished uses a completely smooth pattern [see Figure F15]. **Stamped/Custom** allows you to specify a bitmap for generating the pattern [see Figure F16].

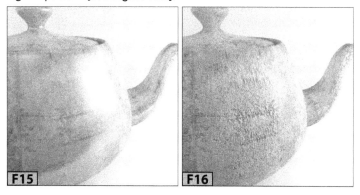

Weathering applies a slight variation in the brightness on the surface of the concrete. The default weathering method is **Automatic** that applies weathering automatically. You can use **Custom** to specify a custom weathering pattern.

Autodesk Generic

This material provides a generic interface for creating a custom appearance. You can convert an Autodesk material to the **Autodesk Generic** material by RMB clicking on the node in the **Slate Material Editor | Active View** and then choosing **Copy as Generic** from the popup menu.

Autodesk Glazing

This material allows you to model a thin and transparent material such as glazing in windows and doors. The **Color** control in the **Glazing** rollout lets you choose the color for the sheet of glass. Figure F17 shows the teapot rendered with the **Blue Green** color applied to it.

Autodesk Harwood

This material is used the model the appearance of a wood. The **Stain** control in the **Wood** rollout allows you to choose a stain to add to the base harwood pattern. Figure F18 shows the wood material with **Brown Stain** color.

The **Finish** control lets you choose the surface finish of the harwood. The **Glossy Varnish** is the default option [see Figure F18]. The other options available are: **Semi-Gloss Varnish** [see Figure F19], **Satin Varnish** [see Figure F20], and **Unfinished** [see Figure F21].

The **Used For** control lets you adjust the appearance of the wood. **Flooring** uses an ocean shader that adds a slight warp to the large surfaces, improving the realism. When you choose **Furniture**, the surfaces are not warped. However, you can use the **Relief Pattern** map to achieve various effects.

When you check **Enable** in the **Relief Pattern** rollout, **mental ray** generates a relief pattern like bump map on the wood surface. The **Type** control lets you choose the relief pattern. When you choose **Based on wood grain**, it generates a relief pattern based on the image map used to create the wood pattern. **Custom** allows you to choose a custom map for the relief pattern. **Amount** lets you adjust the height of the relief pattern.

Autodesk Masonry/CMU

This material can be used to model masonry or concrete masonry units [**CMUs**]. Figure F22 and F23 shows the brick and CMU material.

Autodesk Metal

You can use this material to model various metallic surfaces. The **Type** control in the **Metal** rollout lets you choose the type of material you want to create. These materials define the base color and texture of the material. Figure F24 show the brass material. The **Finish** control lets you choose the surface finish for the surface. Figures F24 and F25 show the brass material with the **Polished** and **Brushed** finish, respectively.

Autodesk Metallic Paint

This material allows you to model a metallic paint surface such as paint of a car [see Figure F26].

Autodesk Mirror

This material lets you model a mirror material [see Figure F27].

Autodesk Plastic/Vinyl

This material allows you to model the surfaces that have a synthetic appearance such as plastic or vinyl [see Figures F28 and F29].

Autodesk Point Cloud Material

This is a special purpose material that is automatically applied to any point-cloud object in the scene. This material allows you to control the overall color intensity, ambient occlusion, and shadows.

Autodesk Solid Glass

This material allows you to model the appearance of the solid glass [see Figure F30].

Autodesk Stone

You can use this material to create the appearance of the stone [see Figures F31 and F32]. The **Type** control in the **Finish Bumps** rollout lets you specify the bump pattern. Available options are: **Polished Granite**, **Stone Wall**, **Glossy Marble**, and **Custom**.

Autodesk Wall Paint

This material can be used to model the appearance of a painted surface such as paint on the walls of a room [see Figures F33 and F34]. The **Application** control in the **Wall Paint** rollout lets you choose the texture method. In other words, you can control how paint is applied on the surface. **Roller** is the default method. Other two methods are **Brush** and **Spray**.

Autodesk Water

This material can be used to model appearance of a water surface [see Figure F35]. The **Type** control in the **Water** rollout lets you choose the scale and texture of the water.

The available options are **Swimming Pool**, **Generic Reflective Pool**, **Generic Stream/River**, **Generic Pond/Lake**, and **Generic Sea/Ocean**. The **Color** control lets you specify the color of the water. This option is only available for **Generic Stream/River**, **Pond/Lake**, and **Sea/Ocean**.

The following options are available for adjusting the color of the water: **Tropical**, **Algae/Green**, **Murky/Brown**, **Generic Reflecting Pool**, **Generic Stream/River**, **Generic Pond/Lake**, **Generic Sea/Ocean** and **Custom**.

Arch & Design Material

The mental ray **Arch & Design** material is a specialized material that allows you to create physically accurate renderings. It is designed to support most of the materials used in the architecture and product design renderings. This material includes self-illumination, ambient occlusion, and advanced options for reflectivity and transparency. It can also round off the sharp corners and edges as a render effect. It is especially fine-tuned for fast glossy reflections and refractions thus improving the workflow and performance.

The **Arch & Design** material has built-in description for all important controls. You can view the details in form of a tooltip. To view the tooltip, hover the cursor over a control's spinner, color swatch, checkbox, and so forth. The **Arch & Design** material attempts to be physically accurate and it outputs a high dynamic range. The visual appeal of the material depends on how colors inside the renderer are mapped to colors displayed on the screen. When you are using the **Arch & Design** material, it is recommended that you use an exposure control such as the **mr Photographic Exposure Control**. When using the **Arch & Design** material, make sure that you use atleast one of the two methods used with **mental ray** for indirect illumination: Final Gathering or Global Illumination. For best results, you can combine final gathering with global illumination. Also, it is recommended that you use physically accurate lights such as **Photometric** lights with the **Arch & Design** material.

To create an **Arch & Design** material, press **M** to open the **Slate Material Editor**. On the **Material/Map Browser | Materials | mental ray** rollout, double-click on **Arch & Design**. The material's interface is displayed in the active view [see Figure F36]. Figure F37 shows a render of teapot with the default **Arch & Design** material applied to it. We will explore the **Arch & Design** material in detail in hands-on exercises.

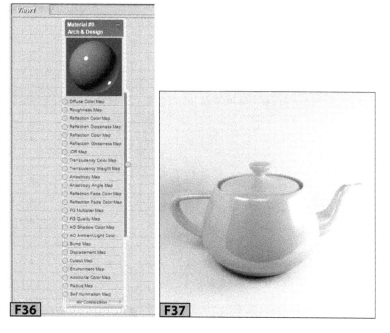

Physical Material

Physical material allows you to model shading effects of the real-world materials with ease. This material is the layered material that gives you ability to efficiently use the physically-based workflows. This material is compatible with **ART** and **mental ray** renderers. Do not use the legacy **Scanline** renderer with it as **Scanline** renderer shows just the approximation of the shader and does not support many crucial features.

This material is comprised of the following:

- A base layer that represents a diffuse color or colored metallic reflections. There can be an option clear-coat layer at the top. The clear-coat layer stays at the top of all layers and reduces energy based on how much energy it reflects and transparency color of the coating.
- Transparency layer
- Sub-surface scattering/translucency layer
- Emission [Self-Illumination] layer. This layer does not participate in the energy conversation and adds energy.

The energy conservation model of this material is somewhat like the **Arch & Design** material. The sum of various shading components can not exceed 100%. One exception is emission, in this case, energy is added. The energy calculation is based on the weight parameters instead of color parameters. This material ensures that the light does not amplify. When the **Metalness** parameter of the material is set to **1**, the material is opaque. It does not produce any Diffuse/Transparency/Sub-surface Scattering effects.

The Physical material comes with number of presets that you can use as a quick starting point. You can select the presets from the **Presets** rollout of the material. The **Material mode** drop-down also in the **Presets** rollout, lets you choose a mode. The two available modes are **Standard** and **Advanced**. The **Advanced** mode is the superset of the **Standard** mode with hidden parameters. In most of the cases, the parameters in the **Standard** mode are sufficient to make physically plausible materials. Some of the advanced parameters are: **Reflection Color** and **Weight**, **Diffuse Roughness**, and controls in the **Advanced Reflectance Parameters** rollout.

Hands-on Exercises

From the **Application** menu, choose **Manage | Set Project Folder** to open the **Browse for Folder** dialog. Navigate to the folder where you want to save the files and then click **Make New Folder**. Create the new folder with the name **unit-mt3** and click **OK** to create the project directory.

Exercise 1: Creating the Leather Material

Let's start by creating a leather material [see Figure E1] using the **Arch & Design** material.

The following table summarizes the exercise.

Table E1: Creating the leather material	
Topics in this section:	• Getting Ready • Creating the Leather Material
Skill Level	Intermediate

Project Folder	unit-mt3
Start File	umt3-hoe1to8-start.max
Final Exercise File	umt3-hoe1-end.max
Time to Complete	20 Minutes

Getting Ready

Open **umt3-hoe1to8-start.max**. Save the scene with the name **umt3-hoe1-end.max**.

Creating the Leather Material

Press **M** to open the **Slate Material Editor**. On the **Material/Map Browser | Materials | mental ray** rollout, double-click on **Arch & Design**. Apply the material to **geo1**, **geo2**, and **geo3** in the scene. On the **Parameter Editor | Templates** rollout, choose **Pearl Finish** from the drop-down. Rename the material as **brownLeatherMat**.

Pearl Finish creates soft blurry reflections without affecting colors or maps. **Matte Finish** allows you to simulate an ideal **Lambertian** shading without affecting the colors or maps. **Glossy Finish** lets you simulate strong reflections without affecting colors or maps.

On the **Main material parameters** rollout, click **Color's** button. On the **Material/Map Browser | Maps | General** rollout, double-click **Bitmap**. On the **Select Bitmap Image File** dialog, choose **brownLeather.jpg**. On the **Gamma** section of the dialog, choose **Override** and set the spinner next to it to **2.2** and then click **Open**.

Tip: General Maps Rollout
*You can also assign diffuse map on the **General Maps** rollout using the **Diffuse Color** option.*

Color controls the color of the surface in direct light. **Diffuse Level** allows you to control the brightness of the diffuse color component. **Roughness** controls the blending of the diffuse component into the ambient component. The **Roughness** values ranges from **0** to **1**. At the **0** value, classical **Lambertian** shading is used. Higher values creates more powdery look.

Tip: Gamma 2.2 Setup
To know more about Gamma 2.2 setup in 3ds Max, visit the following link: http://www.risingpolygon.co/2016/05/gamma-22-setup-linear-workflow-in-3ds.html.

The **Arch & Design** material is energy conserving therefore the actual diffuse level used depends on the reflectivity and transparency. This material makes sure that diffuse+reflection+refraction is less than equal to **1**. The incoming light energy is properly distributed to diffuse, reflection, and refraction components so that it maintains the first law of thermodynamics. If you add reflectivity, the energy must be taken from somewhere, therefore the diffuse and transparency component will be reduced accordingly.

The rules for the energy are as follows:

- **Transparency** takes energy from the diffuse color. If you set transparency to **100%**, there will be no diffuse color.
- **Reflectivity** takes energy from diffuse and transparency, therefore, **100%** reflectivity means there is no diffuse color or transparency on the surface.
- **Translucency** is a type of transparency. The **Translucency Weight** parameter defines the percentage of transparency versus translucency.

On the **brownLeather.jpg | Coordinates** rollout, set **U** and **V** to **0.6** in the **Tiling** column. Also, set **Blur** to **0.2** and take a test render [see Figure E2].

On the **Parameter Editor | brownLeatherMat | Special Purpose Maps** rollout of the material, click **Bump's None** button. On the **Material/Map Browser | Maps | General** rollout, double-click **Bitmap**. On the **Select Bitmap Image File** dialog, choose **brownLeather_bump.jpg**. On the **brownLeather_bump.jpg | Coordinates** rollout, set **U** and **V** to **0.6** in the **Tiling** column. Also, set **Blur** to **0.2**. On the **Special Purpose Maps** rollout of the material, set **Bump** to **0.1** and take a test render [see Figure E3].

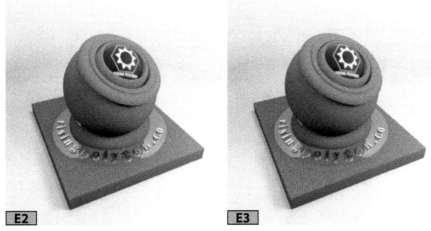

You can use the **Bump** map button to assign a bump map. The strength of the bump can be adjusted using the spinner located on the left of the button. If you turn on **Do not apply bumps to the diffuse shading**, bumps are applied to all components except the diffuse.

On the **Main material parameters** rollout, turn off **Fast (interpolate)** to generate more accurate glossiness.

When **Fast (interpolate)** is on, a smoothing algorithm is used that allows rays to be reused and smoothed. As a result, you get faster and smoother glossy reflections at a cost of accuracy.

When **Highlight + FG only** is turned on, actual rays are not traced in the scene. Only highlights are shown. In addition to this, soft reflections are shown that are produced by final gathering. You can use this option on surfaces that are less essential in the scene. This option works well with surfaces having weak reflections and blurred glossy reflections.

Metal material sets the color of reflection cast by the metallic materials. When **Metal material** is on, the **Color** control defines the color of reflections. The **Reflectivity** control sets the weight between the diffuse reflections and metallic reflections. When off, the **Reflection Color** control defines the color. The **Reflectivity** control plus **BRDF** settings define the intensity and color of the reflections.

Set **Glossiness** to **0.3**. **Glossiness** controls the sharpness of reflection/transparency. The values ranges from **0** [extremely diffuse or blurry transparency] to **1** [completely clear transparency].

Set **Reflectivity** to **0.2** and take a test render [see Figure E4].

Reflectivity controls the overall level of reflectivity. The reflectivity and color values, also known as specular highlight, define the level of reflections and its intensity. **Glossy Samples** specifies the number of rays [samples] **mental ray** shoots in order to calculate the glossy refraction. Higher values produce smooth result at a cost of render time.

Tip: Glossy Samples
A value of 32 is enough for most renderings. If you set Glossy Samples to 1, only one ray is shot, regardless of the actual value of Glossiness. It boosts the rendering performance. You can use it for your test renderings.

On the **BRDF** rollout, make sure **Custom Reflectivity Function** is selected and then set **0 deg. refl** to **0.2** and **Curve shape** to **2**. Now, take a test render [see Figure E5].

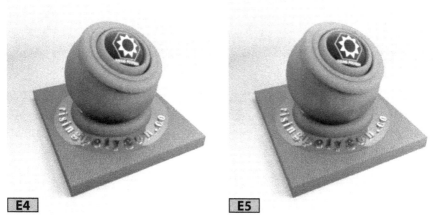

E4 E5

BRDF stands for **Bidirectional Reflectance Distribution Function**. In the real world, the reflectivity of the surface is dependent on the view angle. **BRDF** function allows you to control the reflectivity of the surface based on the angle it is viewed. In real-world surfaces such as glass, water, and other dielectric materials with **Fresnel** effects, the angular dependency of reflection is dependent on **IOR** or index of refraction.

The **Arch & Design** material allows you to set the angular based reflectivity values using **0-degree** faces [surfaces directly facing the camera] and **90-degree** faces [surfaces 90 degrees to the camera]. **Curve Shape** controls the falloff of the BRDF curve. When you choose **By IOR [fresnel reflections]**, the reflectivity is entirely guided by the material's index of refraction.

On the **Fast Glossy Interpolation** rollout, set **Interpolation grid density** to **1** (same as rendering) and take a test render [see Figure E6].

Warning: Interpolation
Interpolation can cause artifacts because it is calculated on the low res grid. It can also cause oversmoothing as it blends neighbors of the low resolution grid. Interpolation works with the flat surfaces. It does not work well with wavy or highly detailed surfaces that uses the bump map.

The controls in the **Fast Glossy Interpolation** rollout can be used to interpolate reflections and refractions thus producing smooth results and improving rendering performance. The interpolation works by pre-calculating glossy reflections in a grid across the image. The number of rays shot by **mental ray** is governed by reflection **Glossy Samples** and refraction **Glossy Samples**.

Press **Ctrl+S** to save the scene with the name **umt3-hoe1-end.max**.

Exercise 2: Creating the Chrome Material

Ok, now we have some knowledge of the **Arch & Design** material. Now, let's create the chrome material [see Figure E1].

The following table summarizes the exercise.

Table E2: Creating the chrome material	
Topics in this section:	• Getting Ready • Creating the Chrome Material
Skill Level	Intermediate
Project Folder	**unit-mt3**
Start File	**umt3-hoe1to8-start.max**
Final Exercise File	**umt3-hoe2-end.max**
Time to Complete	10 Minutes

Getting Ready
Open the **umt3-hoe1to8-start.max**.

Creating the Chrome Material
Apply an **Arch & Design** material to **geo1**, **geo2**, and **geo3** in the scene. On the **Parameter Editor | Main material parameters** rollout | **Diffuse** section, set **Color** to **white**. Setting color to white will create a very highly reflective surface. On the **Reflection** group, set **Reflectivity** to **1**. Also, turn on **Metal material**. Now, take a test render.

Metal material allows you to define the reflection color using the **Diffuse color** parameter.

On the **Refraction** group, set **Color** to **Black** and set **IOR** to **25**.

The **Color** control on the **Refraction** group sets the color of the refraction. You can also use this control to create the colored glass. On the **BRDF** rollout, select **By IOR (fresnel reflections)** and take a render [see Figure E1]. Save the scene with the name **umt3-hoe2-end.max**.

E1

Exercise 3: Creating the Copper Material
Now, let's create the different copper materials [see Figures E1, E5, and E12].

The following table summarizes the exercise.

Table E3: Creating the copper material	
Topics in this section:	• Getting Ready • Creating the Copper Material
Skill Level	Intermediate
Project Folder	**unit-mt3**
Start File	**umt3-hoe1to8-start.max**
Final Exercise File	**umt3-hoe3-end.max**
Time to Complete	20 Minutes

Getting Ready
Open the **umt3-hoe1to8-start.max**. Save the scene with the name **umt3-hoe3-end.max**.

Creating the Copper Material
Let's start with the polished copper material.

Apply an **Arch & Design** material to **geo1**, **geo2**, and **geo3** geometry in the scene. On the **Parameter Editor | Templates** rollout, choose **Glossy Finish** from the drop-down. On the **Parameter Editor | Main material parameters** rollout | **Diffuse** group, set **Color** to the following RGB values: **0.592**, **0.278**, and **0.165**. On the **Reflection** group, set **Reflectivity** to **1** and **Glossiness** to **0.9**. Also, turn on **Metal material**.

On the **Refraction** group, set **IOR** to **1.5**. On the **BRDF** rollout, choose **By IOR (fresnel reflections)** and take a render [see Figure E1].
Now, let's create the copper material with satin finish.

Apply a default **Arch & Design** material to **geo1**, **geo2**, and **geo3** in the scene. On the **Parameter Editor | Main material parameters** rollout | **Diffuse** group, set **Color** to the following RGB values: **0.592**, **0.278**, and **0.165**. On the **Reflection** group, set **Reflectivity** to **0.8** and **Glossiness** to **0.5**. Also, turn on **Metal material**. Take a test render [see Figure E2]. You will see that the material is bright. You need to reduce the brightness of the material.

Set **Diffuse Level** to **0.3** to make the material less bright and take a test render. On the **Anisotropy** rollout, set **Anisotropy** to **0.05** to change the shape of the highlights and take a test render [see Figure E3].

Anisotropy controls the shape of the highlight. At the value **1**, there will be no anisotropy and highlight will be round. At the value **0.01**, the highlight will be elongated. **Rotation** controls the orientation of the highlight. The values for **Rotation** ranges from **0** to **1**, **1** represents **360** degrees.

On the **Reflection** group, set **Glossy Samples** to **16** to increase the quality of the glossiness. On the **BRDF** rollout, set **0 deg. refl** to **0.9** and take a test render [see Figure E4]. Notice in the render that you need to reduce **Glossiness** value.

On the **Reflection** group, set **Glossiness** to **0.4**. On the **Fast Glossy Interpolation** rollout, set **Neighboring points to look up** to **8** and turn on **High detail distance**. Next, set distance to **1** for High detail distance. Now, take a test render [see Figure E5].

Neighboring points to look up lets you set the number of stored grid points are looked up to smooth out the reflective glossiness. The default value for this parameter is **2**. Higher values smear the glossiness. **High detail distance** allows **mental ray** to trace second set of rays to create a clearer version of the glossiness within the specified radius defined by this parameter.

Now, let's create the brushed copper material.

Apply a default **Arch & Design** material to the teapot in the scene. On the **Parameter Editor | Main material parameters** rollout | **Diffuse** group, set **Color** to the following RGB values: **0.592**, **0.278**, and **0.165**. On the **Reflection** group, set **Reflectivity** to **0.5** and **Glossiness** to **0.5** as well. Also, turn on **Metal material**. Now, take a test render [see Figure E6].

Now, we will use the **Noise** map to create brushed metal look in the reflections.

On the **Reflection** group, click **Color** button. On the **Material/Map Browser | Maps | General** rollout, double-click **Noise**. On the **Noise Parameters** rollout, set **Noise Type** as **Fractal** and set **Size** to **1** to create tiny dots in the noise pattern [see Figure E7]. On the **Coordinates** rollout, set **Source** to **Explicit Map Channel**. Also, set **V, V, and W** to **0.5, 100**, and **100** in the **Tiling** column, respectively to create streaks in the noise pattern [see Figure E8].

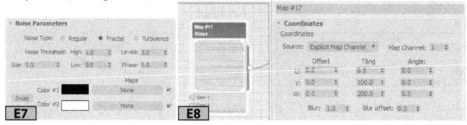

E7   E8

On the **Noise Parameters** rollout, set **Color #1** to medium gray [**Value=122**] and take a test render [see Figure E9]. On the material's **Refraction** group, set **IOR** to **45**. On the **BRDF** rollout, select **By IOR (fresnel reflections)** and take a test render [see Figure E10]. On the **Anisotropy** rollout, set **Anisotropy** to **0.05** to change the shape of the highlights and take a test render [see Figure E11].

E9   E10   E11

Now, I will increase the reflectivity and glossiness values of the surface.

On the material's **Reflection** group, set **Reflectivity** and **Glossiness** to **0.8**. Set **Glossy Samples** to **16**. On the **Fast Glossy Interpolation** rollout, set **Interpolation grid density** to **1/4 (quarter resolution)**, **Neighboring points to look up** to **4**, and turn on **High detail distance**. Next, set distance to **2** for **High detail distance**. Now, take a render [see Figure E12]. Press **Ctrl+S** to save the scene.

Exercise 4: Creating Glass/Thin Plastic film Materials

In this exercise, we're going to create different glass and thin plastic film materials [see Figures E1, E2, E4, E6, E7, and E9]. Let's start with the clear glass material. This material is suitable for solid geometries with some thickness.

E12

The following table summarizes the exercise.

Table E4: Creating the glass/thin plastic film materials	
Topics in this section:	• Getting Ready • Creating Glass/Thin Plastic film Materials
Skill Level	Intermediate
Project Folder	**unit-mt3**
Start File	**umt3-hoe1to8-start.max**
Final Exercise File	**umt3-hoe4-end.max**
Time to Complete	20 Minutes

Getting Ready
Open the **umt3-hoe1to8-start.max**. Save the scene with the name **umt3-hoe4-end.max**.

Creating Glass/Thin Plastic film Materials
Here's the process:

Apply an **Arch & Design** material to **geo1**, **geo2**, and **geo3** in the scene. On the **Parameter Editor | Main material parameters** rollout | **Diffuse** group, set **Color** to **black**. On the **Reflection** group, set **Reflectivity** to **1**. On the **Refraction** group, set **Transparency** to **1** and **IOR** to **1.5**. On the **BRDF** rollout, choose **By IOR (fresnel reflections)** and take a render. On the **Advanced Rendering Options** rollout, set **Max Trace Depth** to **8** in the **Reflections** and **Refraction** groups. Take a test render [see Figure E1].

E1

When the trace depth is equal to the value specified by the **Reflections** group | **Max Trace Depth** control, **mental ray** shows only highlights and emulated reflections created using **Final Gathering**. The material behaves as if **Highlights+FG** is on in the **Main material parameters** rollout | **Reflection** group.

Cutoff Threshold sets a threshold level at which reflections are rejected. The default value for this control is **0.01**. At this value, rays that contribute less than **1%** to the final pixel are ignored.

Max Distance allows you to limit the reflections to a certain distance. It helps in speeding up the rendering as **mental ray** does not include distant objects to glossy reflections. **Fade to end color** lets you fade the reflections to this color. This is suitable for indoor scenes. When this option is turned off, reflections fade to the environment color which is suitable for outdoor scenes.

The optimization settings for the refraction are almost identical to those for reflections. When the trace depth is equal to the value specified by the **Refraction** group | **Max Trace Depth** control, the material refracts black.

Advanced Reflectivity Options group | **Visible area lights cause no Highlights** control, when on, the **mental ray** area lights with **Area Light Parameters** rollout | **Show Icon In Renderer on**, create no specular highlights.

When **Skip reflections on inside (except total internal reflection)** is on, **mental ray** retains total internal reflection [**TIR**]. Most of the reflections inside the transparent objects are very faint except few known as **TIR**. When this option is on, **mental ray** boosts the performance by ignoring the weak reflections but retaining **TIRs**. **Relative Intensity of Highlights** controls the intensity of specular highlights versus the intensity of true reflections.

Next, we will create tinted glass.

On the **Refraction** group, set **Color** to the following RGB values: **0.969**, **0.729**, and **0.659**. Now, take a test render [see Figure E2].

Next, you will create frosted glass.

E2   E3

On the **Refraction** group, set **Transparency** and **Glossiness** to **0.8** and take a test render [see Figure E3]. You will notice that you need to reduce the glossiness farther to make a believable frosted glass. If you reduce the **Glossiness** value, you need to increase samples to compensate. Set **Glossiness** and **Glossy Samples** to **0.5** and **16**, respectively, and take a test render [see Figure E4].

Now, the render is looking much better. Adding a little bit of translucency will make the effect much better so let's do it.

Turn on **Translucency** and set **Weight** to **0.2**. Change **Translucency Color** to the following RGB values: **0.969**, **0.729**, and **0.659** and then take a test render [see Figure E5].

Translucency is a special form of transparency. If you want a material to be translucent, there should exist some transparency in the material. The **Weight** parameter defines how much of the existing transparency is used as translucency. For example, if you set **Weight** to **0.3**, **30** percent of the transparency is used as translucency. It is best suited for thin walled objects such as windows panes or plastic films. **Color** controls the translucency color.

E4   E5

Note: Sub-surface Scattering
*You can create sub-surface scattering effects by using the glossy transparency with the translucency. However, the effect is not as good as created using the dedicated **SSS** shaders.*

On the **Diffuse** group, set **Diffuse Level** to **0.52** to reduce the brightness of the material. Press **Ctrl+S** to save the file.

Next, you will create a glass material that does not include any refraction. This glass is ideal for windows panes with single face.

Open **umt3-hoe4-start.max**. Apply an **Arch & Design** material to the plane geometry in the scene. On the **Parameter Editor | Main material parameters** rollout | **Diffuse** group, set **Color** to black. On the **Reflection** group, set **Reflectivity** to **1**. On the **Refraction** group, set **Transparency** to **1** and **IOR** to **1.5**. On the **BRDF** rollout, choose **By IOR (fresnel reflections)** and take a render.

On the **Refraction** group, set **Color** to the following RGB values: **0.737**, **0.776**, and **0.98**. On the **Advanced Rendering Options** rollout, set **Max Trace Depth** to **8** in the **Reflection** and **Refraction** groups. On the **Advanced Transparency Options** rollout, choose **Thin-walled (can use single face)** for **Glass / Translucency treat objects as**. Now, take a render [see Figure E6].

E6

When you choose **Thin-walled (can use single face)**, the object behaves as if it is made of a very thin sheet of transparent material. On the other hand, **Solid (requires two sides on every object)** tells **mental ray** that the object is made of a solid, transparent substance.

Tip: Creating Magic Walls

Back Face Culling *makes the surfaces invisible to the camera when seen from the reverse side. You can use this option to create magic walls. If you create walls of a room using planes with the normal facing inwards, you can render room from outside. The camera will see into the room, but the wall will still exists and behave normally. For example, they will cast shadows, photon will be bounced off them.*

When you turn off **Transparency propagates Alpha channel**, the transparent objects have an opaque alpha. When on, the alpha-channel information is passed on to the background. The refraction and other transparency effects propagate the alpha of the background "through" the transparent object.

The two parameters in the **Indirect Illumination Options** group are multipliers. **FG/GI multiplier** lets you adjust the material response to the indirect light. **FG Quality** is a local multiplier for the number of final gather rays shot by the material.

Next, you will create a thin blurry plastic material.

Apply the default **Arch & Design** material to the plane geometry in the scene. On the **Parameter Editor | Main material parameters** rollout | **Diffuse** group, set **Color** to white. On the **Reflection** group, set **Reflectivity** to **1**. On the **Refraction** group, set **Transparency** to **0.9**, **Glossiness** to **0.6**, **Glossy Samples** to **16**, and **IOR** to **1.5**. On the **BRDF** rollout, choose **By IOR (fresnel reflections)**.

On the **Advanced Transparency Options** group, choose **Thin-walled (can use single face)** option for **Glass / Translucency treat objects as**. Also, turn on **Transparency propagates Alpha channel** and then take a render [see Figure E7].

If you want to create strong blur, adjust the values of **Transparency** and **Glossiness** in the **Refraction** group. Also, enable **Translucency**. On the **Refraction** group, set **Transparency** to **0.8**, **Glossiness** to **0.8**, and **Glossy Samples** to **16**. Check **Translucency** and set **Weight** to **0.2** and then take a render [see Figure E8].

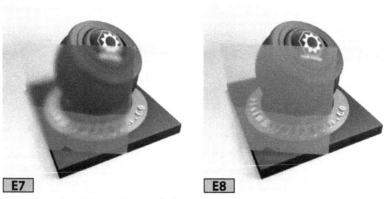

E7   E8

Exercise 5: Creating the Water Material

In this exercise, we are going to create the water material [see Figure E3].

The following table summarizes the exercise.

Table E5: Creating the leather material	
Topics in this section:	• Getting Ready • Creating the Water Material
Skill Level	Intermediate
Project Folder	**unit-mt3**
Start File	**umt3-hoe1to8-start.max**
Final Exercise File	**umt3-hoe5-end.max**
Time to Complete	20 Minutes

Getting Ready
Open the **umt3-hoe1to8-start.max**.

Creating the Water Material
Apply an **Arch & Design** material to **geo1**, **geo2**, and **geo3** in the scene. On the **Parameter Editor | Main material parameters** rollout | **Diffuse** group, set **Color** to the following RGB values: **0.0**, **0.058**, and **0.019**. On the **Reflection** group, set **Reflectivity** to **1**. On the **Refraction** group, set **IOR** to **1.3**. On the **BRDF** rollout, choose **By IOR (fresnel reflections)**. Now, take a test render [see Figure E1].

On the **Special Purpose Maps** rollout of the material, set **Bump** to **0.1** and then click **Bump's None** button. On the **Material/Map Browser | Maps | mental ray** rollout, double-click **Ocean**. Take a test render [see Figure E2].

You need to adjust the values for ocean parameters to get a nice bump. On the **Ocean Parameters** rollout, set **Largest** to **0.5**, **Smallest** to **0.25**, **Quantity** to **3**, and **Steepness** to **1** and then take a render [see Figure E3].

E1 E2 E3

Save the scene with the name **umt3-hoe5-end.max**.

Exercise 6: Creating the Sofa Fabric Material

In this exercise, we're going to create the sofa fabric material [see Figure E1]. The following table summarizes the exercise.

Table E6: Creating the sofa fabric material	
Topics in this section:	• Getting Ready • Creating the Sofa Fabric Material
Skill Level	Intermediate
Project Folder	**unit-mt3**
Start File	**umt3-hoe1to8-start.max**
Final Exercise File	**umt3-hoe6-end.max**
Time to Complete	20 Minutes

Getting Ready
Open the **umt3-hoe1to8-start.max**.

Creating the Sofa Fabric Material

Apply an **Arch & Design** material to the teapot geometry in the scene. Rename the material as **sofaFabricMat**. On the **Main material parameters** rollout, click **Color's** button. On the **Material/Map Browser | Maps | General** rollout, double-click **Bitmap**. On the **Select Bitmap Image File** dialog, choose **sofaFabricDif.jpg**. Also, set gamma override to **2.2**. Also, set **Diffuse Level** to **0.7**.

E1

On the **Coordinates** rollout, set **Blur** to **0.2**. On the **Parameter Editor | sofaFabricMat | Main material parameters** rollout | **Reflection** group, set **Reflectivity** to **0.08**, **Glossiness** to **0.5**, and **Glossy Samples** to **16**. On the **BRDF** rollout, set **0 deg. refl**, **90 deg. refl**, and **Curve shape** to **0.1**, **0.3**, and **2**, respectively. On the **Special Purpose Maps** rollout of the material, click **Bump's None** button. On the **Material/ Map Browser | Maps | General** rollout, double-click **Bitmap**. On the **Select Bitmap Image File** dialog, choose **sofaFabricBump.jpg**.

On the **Coordinates** rollout, set **Blur** to **0.2**. On the **Special Purpose Maps** rollout of the material, set **Bump** to **0.4** and take a render [see Figure E1]. Save the scene with the name **umt3-hoe6-end.max**.

Exercise 7: Creating the Wooden Cabinet Material

In this exercise, we are going to create the wooden cabinet material [see Figure E1].

The following table summarizes the exercise.

Table E7: Creating the leather material	
Topics in this section:	Getting Ready Creating the Wooden Cabinet Material
Skill Level	Intermediate
Project Folder	**unit-mt3**
Start File	**umt3-hoe1to8-start.max**
Final Exercise File	**umt3-hoe7-end.max**
Time to Complete	20 Minutes

Getting Ready
Open the **umt3-hoe1to8-start.max**.

Creating the Wooden Cabinet Material
Apply an **Arch & Design** material to **geo1**, **geo2**, and **geo3** in the scene. Rename the material as **woodCabinetMat**. On the **Main material parameters** rollout | **Diffuse** group, click **Color's** button. On the **Material/Map Browser | Maps | General** rollout, double-click **Bitmap**.

On the Select **Bitmap Image File** dialog, choose **woodCabinetDiff. png**. Also, set gamma override to **2.2**. On the **Coordinates** rollout, set **U** and **V** to **2** in **Tiling** column. Also, set **Blur** to **0.2**. On the **Parameter Editor | woodCabinetMat | Main material parameters** rollout | **Reflection** group, set **Reflectivity** to **0.4**, **Glossiness** to **0.7**, and **Glossy Samples** to **32**. On the **Main material parameters** rollout | **Reflection** group, click **Glossiness** button. On the **Material/Map Browser | Maps | General** rollout, double-click **Bitmap**.

E1

On the **Select Bitmap Image File** dialog, choose **woodCabinetGloss.png**. On the **Coordinates** rollout, set **U** and **V** to **2** in **Tiling** column. Also, set **Blur** to **0.2**. Now, take a test render.

On the **Special Purpose Maps** rollout of the material, click **Bump's None** button. On the **Material/Map Browser | Maps | General** rollout, double-click **Bitmap**. On the **Select Bitmap Image File** dialog, choose **woodCabinetBump.png**. Also, set **U Tiling**, **V Tiling**, and **Blur** values as done earlier.

Take a render [see Figure E1]. Save the scene with the name **umt3-hoe7-end.max**.

Exercise 8: Creating the Parquet Material

In this exercise, we're going to create parquet material for the floor [see Figure E1].

The following table summarizes the exercise.

Table E8: Creating the leather material	
Topics in this section:	• Getting Ready • Creating the Parquet Material
Skill Level	Intermediate
Project Folder	**unit-mt3**
Start File	**umt3-hoe1to8-start.max**
Final Exercise File	**umt3-hoe8-end.max**
Time to Complete	20 Minutes

Getting Ready

Open the **umt3-hoe1to8-start.max**.

Creating the Parquet Material

Apply an **Arch & Design** material to the teapot geometry in the scene. Rename the material as **woodParquetMat**. On the **Main material parameters** rollout | **Diffuse** group, click **Color's** button. On the **Material/Map Browser** | **Maps** | **General** rollout, double-click **Bitmap**. On the **Select Bitmap Image File** dialog, choose **floorParquetDiff.png**. Also, set gamma override to **2.2**.

On the **Coordinates** rollout, set **Blur** to **0.2**. On the **Parameter Editor** | **Main material parameters** rollout | **Reflection** group, set **Reflectivity** to **0.7**, **Glossiness** to **0.7**, and **Glossy Samples** to **16**. On the **Main material parameters** rollout | **Reflection** group, click **Color's** button. On the **Material/Map Browser** | **Maps** | **General** rollout, double-click **Bitmap**. On the **Select Bitmap Image File** dialog, choose **floorParquetRef.png**. On the **Coordinates** rollout, set **Blur** to **0.2**.

E1

On the **Special Purpose Maps** rollout of the material, click **Bump's None** button. On the **Material/Map Browser** | **Maps** | **General** rollout, double-click **Bitmap**. On the **Select Bitmap Image File** dialog, choose **floorParquetBump.png**. On the **Coordinates** rollout, set **Blur** to **0.2**. On the **Special Purpose Maps** rollout of the material, set **Bump** to **0.4** and take a render [see Figure E1].

Save the scene with the name **umt3-hoe8-end.max**.

Exercise 9: Creating Glossy Varnished Wood

In this exercise, we're going to create a varnished glossy wood material using the **Physical** material [see Figure E1].

The following table summarizes the exercise.

Table E9: Creating Glossy Varnished Wood	
Topics in this section:	• Getting Ready • Creating the Material
Skill Level	Intermediate
Project Folder	**unit-mt3**
Start File	**umt3-physical-mat-start.max**
Final Exercise File	**umt3-hoe9-end.max, umt3-hoe9-end-2.max**
Time to Complete	20 Minutes

Getting Ready
Open the **umt3-physical-mat-start**.

Creating the Material
Apply a **Physical** material to the **geo1**, **geo2**, and **geo3** geometries in the scene. Rename the material as **glossyVarnishedMat**. On the **Parameter Editor | Presets** rollout, select **Advanced** from the **Material mode** drop-down. On the **Parameter Editor | glossyVarnishedMat | Basic Parameters** rollout | **Base Color and Reflections** section, click **Base Color's** button.

On the **Material/Map Browser | Maps | General** rollout, double-click **Bitmap**. On the **Select Bitmap Image File** dialog, choose **wooden-plank-1.jpeg**. Also, set gamma override to **2.2**.

The first spinner in the **Base Color and Reflections** section is **Weight**, the relative measurement of the base color. The value in this spinner participate in the energy conversion. Click the button next to **Weight** to assign a map to it.

The Color swatch next to the **Weight** button is the base color of the material. For non-metals, this swatch defines the diffuse color. For metals, it defines the color of the metal itself. Click on the button next to the swatch to assign a color to it.

Take a test render [see Figure E2].

Notice the render in Figure E2, the wood is highly reflective, we need to add some roughness to the reflection and transparency components.

On the **Reflections** section, set **Roughness** to **0.9** and then take a test render [see Figure E3]. Notice that setting **Roughness** to **0.9**, the material has lost its gloss and looks very flat. Glossiness is the effectively the inverse of the roughness. If you enable the **Inv** switch corresponding to the **Roughness** parameter, it will yield glossy material. The **Roughness** parameter lets you control the roughness of the material. A higher **Roughness** value yields a blurrier result. You can lower the **Roughness** value to make the mirror like material.

Enable the **Inv** switch and then set **IOR** to **1.7**.

The **IOR** parameter controls the index of refraction level of the material. If defines how much rays bend when they enter a medium. It also affects the angular dependency of the reflectivity when set to the default **Fresnel** mode [see the **Advanced Reflectance Parameters** rollout].

On the **Transparency** section, click the **Lock** icon and then set **Roughness** to **1**. Also, enable the **Inv** switch. Take a test render [see Figure E4].

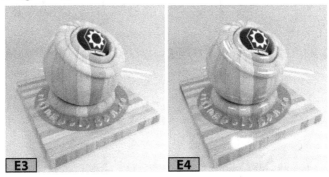

By default, roughness values of reflectivity and transparency are locked together. You can unlink them clicking the **Lock** icon.

On the **Anisotropy** rollout, select **Map channel** and then set **Channel** to **1**. Set **Anisotropy** and **Rotation** to **0.4**, and **0.3**, respectively. Take a test Render [see Figure E5].

The **Anisotropy** parameter controls the U-direction roughness in relation to the V-direction roughness. The **Rotation** parameter controls the anisotropy angle. This control ranges from **0** to **1** which represents one full revolution. The **Auto** option automatically orients the anisotropy whereas the **Map channel** option orients the anisotropy based on a given texture space.

Now, we will create a bump map using the **Noise** map as done in Exercise 3.

Drag a **Noise** map to the active view. On the **Parameter Editor | Noise map | Coordinates** rollout, set **Source** to **Explicit Map Channel** and ensure **Map Channel** is set to **1**. Set **Tiling U, V,** and **W** to **0.5, 200,** and **100,** respectively. On the **Noise Parameters** rollout, set **Size** to **0.2** [see Figure E6].

Set **Color #1** to **RGB[180, 180, 180]**. Drag a **Mix** map to the active view. Connect **Noise** map to the **Color 1** port of the **Mix** map and **Bitmap** to the **Color 2** port. Connect the **Mix** map to the **Bump Map** port of **glossyVarnishedMat** [see Figure E7]. On the **Parameter Editor | Mix** map | **Mix Parameters** rollout, set **Mix Amount** to **30**.

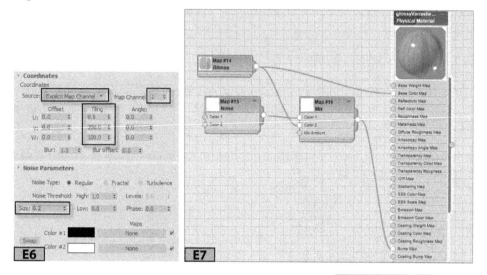

E6

E7

Take the final render [see Figure E1]. Now, if you want to create a less glossy satin varnished wood material, you need to lower down the reflection **Roughness** and **IOR** values [see Figure E8].

Check the **umt3-hoe9-end-2.max** file for the satin varnished material.

Exercise 10: Creating Glass Materials

In this exercise, we're going to create a glass materials using the **Physical** material.

The following table summarizes the exercise.

E8

Table E10: Creating the Glass Materials	
Topics in this section:	• Getting Ready • Creating the Materials
Skill Level	Intermediate
Project Folder	**unit-mt3**
Start File	**umt3-physical-mat-start.max**
Final Exercise File	**umt3-hoe10-end.max**
Time to Complete	20 Minutes

Getting Ready
Open the **umt3-physical-mat-start.max** file.

Creating the Materials
Apply a **Physical** material to **Geo1**, **Geo2**, and **Geo3** in the scene. Rename the material as **glassMat**. On the **Parameter Editor | glassMat** material | **Presets** rollout, choose **Advanced** from the **Material mode** drop-down.

There are two types of modes available for the **Physical** material: **Standard** and **Advanced**. When you choose the **Standard** mode, you get access to the parameters that you can use to create most physically plausible materials. The **Advanced** mode gives you access to advanced reflection, roughness, and weight parameters. You can use these parameters to create advanced materials.

On the **glassMat** material | **Basic Parameters** rollout | **Base Color** section, set **Base Color** weight to **0**. The material turns black. On the **Transparency** section, set the **Transparency** weight to **1** to make the glass completely transparent [see Figure E1]. On the **Reflections** section, set **IOR** to **1.7**.

The **IOR** value sets the Index of **Refraction** level. It controls how much rays bend when entering in a medium.

Turn on the **Thin-walled** box and take a test render [see Figure E2].

When this box is turned on, the object is considered to be made out of an infinitelly thin transparent shell. This shell us not reflective. Also, the transparency depth is disabled and the sub-surface scattering is replaced by translucency.

Turn off the **Thin-walled** box.

You can create tinted glass by specifying a color for **Transparency** and specifying a depth. In the **Transparency** section, set color to **Red** and then set **Depth** to **0.05** and take a render [see Figure E3].

You can create some interesting effects by using sub-surface scattering option. On the **Sub-Surface Scattering** section, set color to yellow and take a test render. Notice that there is no change in the color of the glass. As discussed earlier, the sum of various shading components can not exceed 100%, therefore, you need to reduce weight of other parameter to see the effect of sub-surface scattering.

On the **Transparency** section, set **weight** to **0.85** and take a render [see Figure E4].

Exercise 11: Creating Metal Materials

In this exercise, we're going to create a metal materials using the **Physical** material.

The following table summarizes the exercise.

Table E11: Creating the Metal Materials	
Topics in this section:	• Getting Ready • Creating the Materials
Skill Level	Intermediate
Project Folder	**unit-mt3**
Start File	**umt3-physical-mat-start.max**
Final Exercise File	**umt3-hoe11-end.max**
Time to Complete	20 Minutes

Getting Ready
Open the **umt3-physical-mat-start.max** file.

Creating the Materials
Apply a **Physical** material to **Geo1**, **Geo2**, and **Geo3** in the scene. Rename the material as **metalMat**. On the **Parameter Editor** | **glassMat** material | **Presets** rollout, choose **Advanced** from the **Material mode** drop-down.

First, we will create highly reflective material. On the **glassMat** material | **Basic Parameters** rollout | **Base Color** section, set **Base Color** weight to **0**. On the **Reflections** section, set **IOR** to **48** and then take a test render [see Figure E1]. The reflection in the material is coming from the gray background. If you want more reflections in the metal, use a reflection map.

Now, if you want to create a material like aluminium, blur the reflections by adding some roughness to the metal. On the **Reflections** section, set **Roughness** to **0.3** and take a render [see Figure E2]. You can make the metal darker by darkening the **Reflection** color. Set it to medium gray and take a render [see Figure E3].

If you want to add of the weight of the base color to the material, it will have no effect because of the high **IOR** value. If you use low **IOR** values, you loose the metal look. To compensate for this, you can use the **Metalness** parameter. If you set **Metalness** to **1**, you do not see the base layer, just the colored reflections.

On the **Parameter Editor** | **metalMat** | **Basic Parameters** rollout | **Base Color** section, set base color to **RGB[0.82, 0.416, and 0.099]** and weight to **0.3**. On the **Reflections** section, set reflection color to **RGB[0.584, 0.584, 0.584]**, weight to **0.7**, **Roughness** to **0.3**, **Metalness** to **0.5**, and **IOR** to **6**. Take a render [see Figure E4].

Summary
The unit covered the following topics:

- Autodesk Materials
- Arch & Design Material
- Physical Material

Index

This page is intentionally left blank

Other Books Published by Rising Polygon

Rising Polygon Publishing

[Best Textbooks at Lower Prices]

Modeling Techniques
with
3ds Max 2016 and CINEMA 4D R17 Studio
The Ultimate Beginner's Guide

@risingpolygon
www.risingpolygon.co

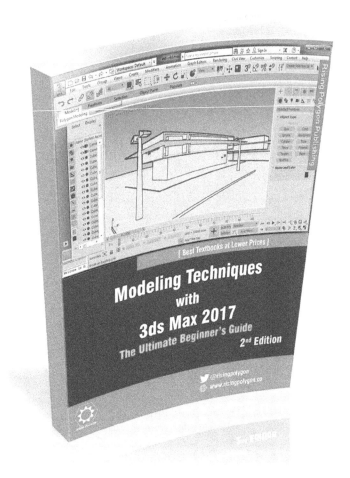

[Best Textbooks at Lower Prices]

Modeling Techniques
with
3ds Max 2017
The Ultimate Beginner's Guide
2nd Edition

@risingpolygon
www.risingpolygon.co

[Best Textbooks at Lower Prices]

Modeling Techniques
with
CINEMA 4D R17 Studio
The Ultimate Beginner's Guide
2nd Edition

@risingpolygon
www.risingpolygon.co

Modeling Techniques

with

3ds Max 2017 and CINEMA 4D R17 Studio

The Ultimate Beginner's Guide

2ⁿᵈ Edition

@risingpolygon
www.risingpolygon.co

Texturing Techniques
with
3ds Max 2017
The Ultimate Beginner's Guide

* Contains 3 bonus chapters on creating cutsom maps and textures using Photoshop.

@risingpolygon
www.risingpolygon.co

Best Textbooks at Lower Prices

Rising Polygon Publishing

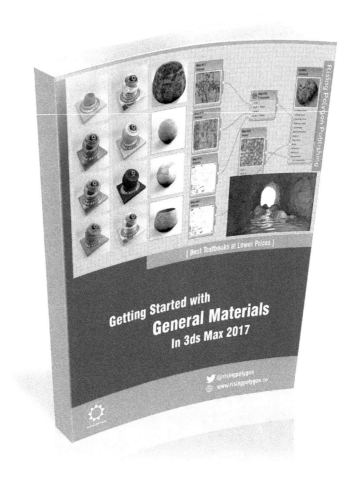

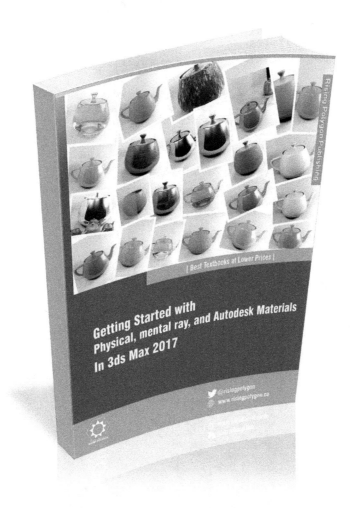

Getting Started with
Physical, mental ray, and Autodesk Materials
In 3ds Max 2017

@risingpolygon
www.risingpolygon.co

| Best Textbooks at Lower Prices |

Rising Polygon Publishing

[Best Textbooks at Lower Prices]

Modeling and Texturing Techniques

With

3ds Max 2017

The Ultimate Beginner's Guide

The Ultimate Beginner's Guide

* Contains 3 bonus chapters on creating cutsom maps and textures using Photoshop.

@risingpolygon
www.risingpolygon.co

www.ingramcontent.com/pod-product-compliance
Lightning Source LLC
LaVergne TN
LVHW062315060326
832902LV00013B/2237